*It is remarkable how closely the history
of the apple tree is connected with that of man.*
Henry David Thoreau

# APPLE ORCHARD COOK BOOK

Janet M. Christensen
and Betty Bergman Levin

THE BERKSHIRE TRAVELLER PRESS
Stockbridge, Massachusetts, 01262

A FEW OTHER BERKSHIRE TRAVELLER BOOKS:

Country Inns and Back Roads, North America
Country Inns and Back Roads, Europe
The Country Inn Cookbook
Treasured Recipes of Country Inns
A Book Of Practical Barn Plans

8 7 6

Library of Congress #78-060319
ISBN 0-912944-49-8
Copyright 1978 Janet Christensen and Betty Bergman Levin
Printed in U.S.A.

COVER PAINTING: Terrence Fehr

Printed in Dalton, Massachusetts by The Studley Press

Dedicated to
Mom
and the
American Flag!

# ACKNOWLEDGMENTS

The authors are grateful to the New York/New England Apple Institute for the assistance which aided in the preparation of this book. In addition, the following people and organizations helped with their ideas and encouragement:

Guy Paris and the Massachusetts Department of Food and Agriculture

The International Apple Institute

Margaret Spader, J. Walter Thompson Co., New York

Mildred Worthen Christensen

Charlotte King

"Good Day!" seen on WCVB-TV, Boston, and on the New England Network whose 1974 New England Apple Cook-Off, which was co-sponsored with the New England states' Departments of Agriculture, resulted in some of the award-winning recipes in this collection.

# APPLE ORCHARD COOKBOOK INGREDIENTS

# AN APPLE-LOGUE

Apples are a favorite American symbol representing home, hearth, and happiness. The legends and lore about the round, red fruit have filled volumes. Whether eaten freshly picked from a tree or cooked in any manner of ways, they are as much a staple of the American diet as hamburgers, fried chicken, or baked potatoes. Their good taste, general availability, moderate price, and extreme versatility contribute to their popularity; the fact that they are also nutritious comes as a bonus.

While memories of backyard apple trees belong primarily to an earlier generation, more than ever, people are compensating for urban lifestyles by taking autumn treks to rural areas to select orchard-fresh apples. With a growing consciousness about ecology and health in recent years, these weekend excursions have increased in popularity. More and more families are marching to the roadside stands, and even straight into the orchards to pay for the privilege and experience of picking their own Macs and Cortlands.

What to do with the bounty!? Simple . . . start cooking! Bake, slice, blend, grate, sauté, simmer, broil. The list goes on! This collection of one hundred and one kitchen-tested apple recipes is designed to cover that broad range of possibilities from familiar sauces, cakes, and pies to the more exotic soufflés, kuchens, and candies. Many of the recipes can be made and frozen for later use.

This book is a result of countless hours of mulling over and cooking apple recipes, many of which were entries in several years' worth of apple cooking contests; dozens of them are actually those award-winning selections. In addition to extending your own list of apple recipes, you can include your own family favorites on the blank pages at the end of the book and create a personalized cookbook to be coveted by future generations.

The authors hope that by providing a selection of apple information . . . quotes and quips . . . statistics and tips . . . that there will also be a large measure of enjoyment and amusement in using this *Apple Orchard Cookbook.*

# APPLE PICKINGS

## AVAILABILITY

| | |
|---|---|
| July to August | Early McIntosh, Gravenstein, Yellow Transparent |
| August to November | Wealthy |
| September to December | Grimes Golden |
| September to June | Jonathan, Late McIntosh |
| October to May | Red Delicious, Golden Delicious, Cortland, York Imperial, Rhode Island Greening |
| October to April | Newtown Pippin, Baldwin, Rome Beauty |
| November to March | Northern Spy, Stayman, |
| November to May | Winesap |

## USES

**All-purpose: eating, salads, and most cooking**

| | |
|---|---|
| Yellow Transparent | Northern Spy |
| Baldwin | Wealthy |
| Jonathan | McIntosh |
| Stayman | Gravenstein |
| Winesap | Grimes Golden |
| York Imperial | Rhode Island Greening |
| Cortland | Golden Delicious |

**Eating**

| | |
|---|---|
| Delicious, Red | Northern Spy |
| Delicious, Golden | Wealthy |
| Newtown Pippin | McIntosh |

**Baking**

| | |
|---|---|
| Cortland | Baldwin |
| Stayman | Rome Beauty |
| Winesap | |

# A BASKETFUL OF VARIETIES

CORTLAND

*Usually a medium to large apple, somewhat flat, oval in shape; bright red with some green and yellow. The flesh is firm, white, and the jacket thin. Particularly good for fresh salad uses as the white retains its color longer than other varieties. It's mildly aromatic, mildly acid, and delicate in texture. Excellent for eating, good for baking, and fine for pies and sauces.*

GOLDEN DELICIOUS

*Generally medium to large with a yellow jacket that is sometimes yellow/green. The stem end is full and round, tapering slightly toward the blossom end, resulting in an elongated oval shape. The velvety skin occasionally has a russet appearance. Flesh is yellowish, fine-grained, mildly aromatic. It's crisp and tender and tastes sweet and juicy, not acidy. Holds its color without browning when exposed to air and is rarely mealy, even when overripe. Good for all uses.*

JONATHAN

*Small to medium in size, solid bright to dark red in color. Slightly tough, thin skin with occasional red veins through yellowish, white flesh. Crisp, tender, juicy, very aromatic, moderately tart, and sprightly in flavor. An all-purpose apple.*

McINTOSH

*Most frequently, a medium sized apple, fairly symmetrical in shape. The bright red color with occasional greenish yellow stripes radiates from the stem end or sometimes has a green undertone with large blushed areas of red. This is a thin-skinned apple and the skin separates readily from the flesh, but the skin itself is moderately tough. Inside, the flesh is whitish yellow with occasional faint red veins. It's juicy, crisp, medium acid, very aromatic, and flavorful. A good all-purpose apple, very tender. When cooking, be cautious not to overcook.*

NEWTOWN PIPPIN

*Available mostly on the West Coast; is medium to large in size with angular oval shape; deep green to yellow/green color, often slightly russeted. Slightly coarse texture, crisp, moderately tart. A good "keeper" which is excellent for cooking. Used a great deal for commercial processing.*

## NORTHWEST GREENING and RHODE ISLAND GREENING
*Available in East and Midwest. Medium to large in size, angular oval shape, moderately tart with firm, crisp texture. First becomes available in October, good for cooking and baking and fair for fresh eating. Utilized by the processing industry.*

## RED DELICIOUS
*Skin is thin, smooth, and protective. The stem end is full and round. It tapers toward the blossom end. Note five distinct "knobs" on the calyx or blossom end — an exclusive for Delicious. Range in color from light red with bold stripes and tinges of yellow/green to brilliant red and dark red. The flesh is creamy white and fine-grained; it's sweet, crisp, and juicy with a mild aroma. It's a low acid apple. The color of the flesh oxidizes when exposed to air. Its sweetness, flavor, and juiciness make it a good eating and snacking apple.*

## ROME BEAUTY
*Medium to quite large in size. Good basic red color occasionally with greenish yellow stripes. Skin is thick, touch, and smooth. Feels firm and heavy. Flesh is whitish yellow. Taste medium acid; agreeably mild. Cooking or baking improves flavor. Holds shape well during cooking; fair for eating. for eating.*

## STAYMAN
*Generally medium to large in size. Slightly elongated oval shape; deep red in color, often with some green undertone showing on the surface. Usually slightly russeted which does not affect quality. Moderately tart, full, rich flavor. An excellent all-purpose apple for eating, cooking, or baking.*

## WINESAP
*A solid, small to medium, deep red apple. Sometimes looks as if the dark red were lavishly splashed over a yellow/green ground color. The skin is medium thick, leathery, and somewhat oily – which makes it a good keeper. Inside flesh is yellow with occasional red veins. Has a coarse, firm texture and spicy aroma, with a sprightly, medium acid, winey taste — good for eating or cooking.*

## YORK IMPERIAL
*Medium to large in size, blushed, light to pinkish red and green in color. Shape is lopsided. Skin thick and bright. Flesh yellowish in color, firm, crisp, and coarse textured. Taste mildly tart, used primarily for commercial processing.*

# A TIME FOR TASTING

Wine and cheese tasting parties have increased people's interests and tastebuds in discerning the minor differences within groups of foods. Apples lend themselves to a unique taste test that has all the makings of a terrific party. Serve apple drinks, appetizers, and desserts to complement the theme. Copy the information on the various characteristics and place on cards along with a plate of each variety of apple. To proceed with the taste test, do the following:

1. Place one whole apple of each variety on a large plate.
2. Cut another apple of the same variety in 8 to 10 pieces. Place on the same plate.
3. Look at the whole apple, noting size, shape, color, symmetry. Smell the apple, waft it gently under your nose. Does it have a characteristic aroma?
4. Look at the cut apples noting color of flesh. Snowy white? Creamy? Translucent? Is the peel thick? Leathery? Thin?
5. Bite into a slice of each variety. Is it tart? Savor the juice. Is it sweet? Slightly sour? Is the skin tender or tough?
6. What about texture? Is it tender? Crisp? Mellow? Mealy? Hard?
7. Which variety has the most flavor? Which has the most aroma?
8. Note color of cut slices after they have been exposed to the air for a few minutes. Does the flesh of some varieties stay white longer than others?
9. Which varieties would be best for salads and fruit cups? Which would you like to serve with meat dishes? Which for desserts?
10. Which varieties would combine best for flavorful pies and sauce?
11. Which variety do you prefer to eat out of hand?

# APPLE AREAS

If you want to go apple-picking, check with your state Department of Agriculture which can usually provide a complete list of orchards that are open to the public for apple-picking. Availability of labor and that year's crop may determine just how much and to what extent a particular orchard is open, so invest in a call ahead of time so as not to be disappointed after driving long distances. Prices will vary depending on market demand, but without question, it's a fun day's activity for the whole family.

The following list indicates those parts of the country which produce the major portion of apples available. An average apple crop in the United States is about 160 million bushels and increasing annually. In a normal year, the following relationship would exist:

**Washington** — 27,500,000 bushels. Leading varieties: Delicious, Winesap, and Golden Delicious.

**The Appalachian Area** (Virginia, Pennsylvania, West Virginia, and Maryland) — 26,000,000 bushels. Leading varieties: York Imperial, Delicious, Stayman, Rome, Golden Delicious, Jonathan, and Winesap.

**New York** — 21,000,000 bushels. Leading varieties: McIntosh, Rhode Island Greening, Delicious, Cortland, Rome, Baldwin, Northern Spy, and Golden Delicious.

**Michigan** — 15,000,000 bushels. Leading varieties: Jonathan, McIntosh, Northern Spy, Delicious, Golden Delicious, and Rome.

**California** — 10,000,000 bushels. Leading varieties: Yellow Newtown, Gravenstein (summer apple), Delicious, Rome, Golden Delicious, and Jonathan.

**New England** — 8,500,000 bushels. Leading varieties: McIntosh, Cortland, Delicious, Ida Red, and Spartan.

**Ohio, Indiana, and Illinois** — 6,500,000 bushels. Leading varieties: Jonathan, Rome, Golden Delicious, Stayman, and Delicious.

**New Jersey** — 3,000,000 bushels. Leading varieties: Rome, Delicious, Stayman, and Starr (summer apple).

**North Carolina** — 3,000,000 bushels. Leading varieties: Rome, Delicious, Stayman, and Golden Delicious.

**Oregon** — 2,500,000 bushels. Leading varieties: Yellow Newtown, Delicious, and Golden Delicious.

**Idaho and Colorado** — 3,000,000 bushels. Leading varieties: Delicious, Rome, Jonathan, and Winesap.

# APPLE TREATS

Americans love to eat apples by sinking their teeth into the sweet juicy fruit; Europeans prefer to use a fruit knife, slice and then enjoy. When cooking with apples, instructions frequently call for sliced or diced apples. The following suggestions simplify the choice.

To slice an apple efficiently, the blossom end of the apple (opposite from the stem) should be cut out first. Then, cut several thin slices parallel to the core, down to the core. Continue slicing wedges around the apple. For pies, peel the apple first; for fried apples, leave unpeeled.

When eating fresh or slicing for applesauce, use an apple slicer-corer. The "fancy gadget," which isn't really so fancy, is quick, simple, and can usually be purchased for under a dollar. (When making applesauce, a Foley food mill is invaluable to get an even consistency. Many of the more expensive food processors will do the same, but be careful not to over-process and liquidize the sauce.)

To dice an apple, cut the apple to the core every half-inch, vertically. Turn the apple and cut to the core every half-inch horizontally. Slice through the apple to form cubes about a half-inch or less. The above steps will use from one-third to one-half of the apple. Repeat the first steps for the remainder of the apple. This method for the use of diced apples is good for lumpy applesauce, salads, and other specified recipes.

The English "starcut" is recommended when apple slices are to be served for dipping or simply eating raw. For attractive one-bite segments of apple, hold the apple and slice through *horizontally*. You will now have two halves with core cross-sectioned usually showing the pattern of a five-branch star. Divide each half into 5, cutting along one of the branches to the center, then along an adjacent branch so each segment is removed. Pare out the core line from the top of each segment without wasting any of the flesh. The five bite-sized pieces are perfect for decorative arrangements, in salads, or for fondue dipping.

## CANNING APPLES OR SAUCE

Well worth the effort! Cut pared and cored apples into pieces. (To keep from darkening, place in solution of 2 tablespoons each of salt and vinegar to one gallon of water.) Drain and then boil 5 minutes in thin sugar syrup or water. Pack hot fruit in sterilized glass jars to ½-inch of top; cover with hot syrup or water, leaving ½-inch space at top of jar. Adjust jar lids and process in boiling-water bath (212 degrees F.), 15 minutes for pint jars or 20 minutes for quart jars. As soon as jars are removed from boiling water, complete seals if necessary.

To can applesauce: Heat sweetened or unsweetened homemade applesauce to simmering (185 to 210 degrees F.), stirring to keep from sticking. Pack hot applesauce in sterilized glass jars to ¼-inch of top; adjust lids. Process in boiling-water bath (212 degrees F.), 10 minutes for pint jars or quart jars. As soon as jars are removed from boiling water, complete seals if necessary.

## THRIFTY APPLE SKIN JELLY

Use every bit of the orchard bounty! When paring apples for pie, sauce, or other dishes, discard stem and blossom ends or any bad spots; place skins and cores in saucepan. Add 1 cup cold water, cook over low heat for 25 minutes and strain juice into cup. (From 4 apples, there should be about ¼ cup.) If there is too much juice, boil it down to ¼ cup; if too little, add water to skins until just ¼ cup juice is obtained. Return juice to saucepan and add 3 tablespoons sugar; stir over low heat till sugar is dissolved. Boil rapidly 1 to 2 minutes, testing constantly until jelly sheets from a spoon. Turn into a glass jar, or use as glaze for an open pie or tart. (If you make a larger quantity or want to store this jelly, pour into hot sterilized jars and seal with paraffin.)

## FREEZING APPLES

It's easy! Core and peel apples. Slice into twelfths or sixteenths directly into a brine solution of 2 tablespoons salt to one gallon cold water. Blanch in steam for 90 seconds (preferred method), or in boiling water for 60 seconds. Chill in cold water; drain. Sprinkle ½ cup sugar evenly over each quart (about 1½ lbs.) apples; stir and let stand until sugar is dissolved. Pack into containers, leaving about ½-inch space under cover. Freeze.

## APPLE LEATHER (A Dried "Fruit Roll")

A delectable snack! Use ripe or overripe apples; peel if desired, then core and cut in chunks. Puree in food chopper or blender. For a lighter color, add one tablespoon of lemon or lime juice for each quart of fruit. Line a cookie sheet or tray with waxed paper and pour in the blended fruit about ¼ inch deep. Set oven at its lowest temperature (140 degrees); place trays inside and leave the oven door open from 2 to 6 inches. The apple leather will be dried in 4 to 5 hours. Enjoy as a snack, or create a beverage by adding 5 parts water to 1 part apple leather in a blender.

# APPLE~TIZERS

Dips and Hors d'Oeuvres
Soups and Beverages
Snacks

# APPLE DIPPER

**8-ounce pkg. cream cheese, softened**
**3 or 4 tablespoons apple juice or cider**
**½ cup grated apples**
**2 teaspoons chopped chives**
**Dash of salt**

1. Combine cream cheese and apple juice until smooth and creamy. Blend in well the grated apples; stir in chives and salt to taste. Chill.

2. Serve with carrot and celery sticks, radish roses, apple wedges, and other fresh fruit, vegetables, and crackers as desired.
   Makes about 1½ cups dip.

*Carbonized remains of apples have been found by archeologists in pre-historic lake dwellings in Switzerland and are presumed to be a relic of the Iron Age.*

# FRUIT CURRY DIP

2 cups dairy sour cream
¾ cup (8 or 9 oz. can) crushed pineapple, drained
⅔ cup chopped red apples
1 teaspoon curry powder
½ teaspoon garlic salt
Apple slices for garnish

1. Blend sour cream with pineapple, apple, curry powder, and garlic salt.

2. Chill. Garnish with sliced apples around edge of bowl. Especially good with shredded wheat wafers. Makes about 3 cups.

*In Herefordshire, Devonshire, and Cornwall, England, the old custom of "Wassailing" the apple orchards on Christmas Eve still persists. The farmers walk in procession to a chosen tree in each orchard where an incantation is spoken and a bowl of cider dashed against the trunk of the tree, thus ensuring a fruitful harvest.*

# SAUSAGE AND APPLE APPETEASERS

8-ounce pkg. Crescent Dinner Rolls
2 tablespoons melted butter
2 medium apples, pared, cored, and chopped fine
6 slices bacon, cooked until crisp and crumbled
8 Brown and Serve Sausage Links

1. Preheat oven to 375 degrees. Separate dough into 4 rectangles, press perforation to seal. Brush each with butter.

2. Combine finely chopped apple and bacon bits. Spread some of the mixture over dough. Cut each rectangle crosswise to form 2 squares. Place a sausage link on each square; roll up. Cut each roll into 3 or 4 bite size pieces, secure with wooden toothpick. Place cut side down on ungreased cookie sheet.

3. Bake 12 to 15 minutes until golden brown. Makes 24 to 32 appetizers.

*Note:* If you do not wish to cut the rolls they can be used as sandwich size.


*Don't pluck a green apple; when it is ripe it will fall itself.*
Russian Proverb

# SWEDISH HAM BALLS
# IN BROWN SAUCE

2½ pounds ground ham
1 cup chopped, peeled apples
2 cups bread crumbs
2 eggs, well beaten
¾ cup milk
1 cup brown sugar
1 teaspoon dry mustard
½ cup vinegar
½ cup water

1. Combine ham, apples, crumbs, eggs, and milk in a large bowl; mix thoroughly. Form into small balls and place in 9 x 13-inch baking pan.

2. Mix together remaining ingredients; stir until sugar dissolves. Pour sauce over ham balls.

3. Bake at 325 degrees for one hour. Baste frequently. Makes 5 dozen hors d'oeuvre size ham balls, or 32 large size.

# ZESTY HORS D'OEUVRE

**4 slices lean bacon**
**3-ounce pkg. cream cheese**
**¼ cup crumbled blue cheese**
**½ cup cornflake crumbs**
**1 cup finely chopped apples**
**¼ teaspoon sugar**
**¼ teaspoon cinnamon**
**¼ cup ground walnuts**

1. Fry bacon until crisp. Chop into small pieces; set aside. Mix together cream cheese and blue cheese. Add ¼ cup cornflake crumbs and the apple, sugar, cinnamon, walnuts, and bacon; mix well.

2. Shape into small balls. Roll balls in remaining cornflake crumbs. Chill until serving. Serve on toothpicks. Makes about 20 balls.

*The signers of the Declaration of Independence toasted their achievement with apple cider and brandy from orchards already a century and a half old.*

# CURRIED APPLE AND BANANA SOUP

2½ cups vegetable stock*
3 to 4 apples, cored, peeled, and coarsely grated
1 large very ripe banana, peeled
1 onion, coarsely chopped
1 tablespoon curry powder
Pinch of salt
1 large potato, peeled, and finely diced
1 pint light cream, scalded
Chopped chives

1. Place 1¼ cups of the vegetable stock in blender
   with apples, banana, onion, curry powder, and
   salt. Blend to smooth puree.

2. In a large saucepan, combine the puree, potato,
   and remaining stock. Bring to a boil; reduce heat
   and simmer, covered, 15 minutes or until potato
   is tender. While soup is cooking, scald cream.

3. Place soup in blender and blend until as smooth
   as possible. Add cream to soup, pouring it
   through a sieve. Stir to blend. Chill. Garnish
   with chives. Makes about 6 cups or 10 to
   12 servings.

*Note:* If you do not have a blender, use a food mill
or sieve.

*For 1 gallon homemade vegetable stock: Combine 5 stalks
celery, diced, 3 large carrots (with tops if possible), diced,
1 large onion with skin, quartered, 3 parsnips, sliced, with 2
gallons water in large pot. Add one bunch each of fresh
parsley and dill (or substitute parsley flakes and dill seed).
Bring to a boil; simmer, covered, 1 hour or until reduced one
half. Strain.

# SUPERB SCANDINAVIAN APPLE SOUP

3 cups diced apples
2 cups chicken broth
½ teaspoon cinnamon
Dash of salt
½ cup sugar
½ cup sweet red wine
1 tablespoon cornstarch
½ cup sweet red wine
3 or 4 drops red food coloring (optional)
Whipped cream
Cinnamon

1. Simmer, covered, the diced apples, chicken broth, cinnamon, and salt until apples are soft, about 25 minutes. Mash through a strainer. Add sugar, red wine, and food coloring.

2. Taste for sweetness (depends on apples used) and add more wine or sugar if needed.
   Chill well.

3. Top each serving with a dab of whipped cream and sprinkle with cinnamon.
   Makes 4 to 6 servings.

*Nearly all apples available after harvest time in the fall come from refrigerated storages.*

# APPLE NECTAR

¾ cup apple juice
1 egg, separated
¼ cup water
¾ cup milk
1 tablespoon sugar
1 tablespoon lemon juice
1 tablespoon honey
Dash of nutmeg

1. Put all the ingredients, except the egg white and the nutmeg, into a blender and blend until well mixed, or combine with rotary beater.

2. Fold in the stiffly beaten egg white and very lightly sprinkle the top with nutmeg.
   Makes 2 cups.

*Of Jonathan Chapman*
*Two things are known,*
*That he loved apples,*
*That he walked alone.*
Rosemary and Stephen St. Vincent Benet,
*Johnny Appleseed*

# MULLED CIDER

**1 quart apple cider or apple juice**
**1 teaspoon whole allspice**
**1 teaspoon whole cloves**
**2 sticks cinnamon**
**6 thin lemon slices, if desired**

1. Combine ingredients, except lemon slices, in a saucepan. Simmer covered for 20 minutes.

2. Remove spices. Serve hot with lemon slices, if desired. Makes 6 servings.

*Planting the trees/that would march and train*
*On in his name/to the great Pacific,*
*Like Birnam Wood/to Dunsinane,*
*Johnny Appleseed*
*Swept on.*
Nicholas Vachel Lindsay
*In Praise of Johnny Appleseed*

# APPLE CINNAMON CHEESIES

2 pkgs. (8 oz. each) Crescent Dinner Rolls
4 slices American cheese
3 McIntosh apples
3 tablespoons sugar
1 teaspoon cinnamon

1. On a cookie sheet, separate rolls as directed. On each triangle (near bottom), lay a small piece of cheese. Next, peel and slice apples very thin; place slices on top of cheese.

2. Combine sugar and cinnamon and sprinkle mixture over each. Roll up gently as you would normally.

3. Bake at 350 degrees for 15 or 20 minutes or until golden brown. Makes 16 servings.

*Apples have been known to help insomniacs. When you can't fall back to sleep, try an apple; it'll take the blood from the brain and result in restful sleep.*

# CHEESE APPLETIZERS

*Pastry:*
**2 cups (8 oz.) grated sharp Cheddar cheese**
**1 cup (2 sticks) butter or margarine**
**2½ cups flour**
*Filling:*
**6 cups pared, chopped apples**
**½ cup granulated sugar**
**½ cup light brown sugar, firmly packed**
**1 tablespoon frozen orange juice concentrate**
**⅓ cup flour**

1. Have cheese and butter at room temperature. Cream until smooth; gradually add flour and mix well. Shape dough into 4 balls and wrap; chill.

2. To make filling: combine all ingredients in saucepan. Cook over low heat until thickened. Cool before using.

3. On floured board, roll each section into a 12 x 6-inch rectangle. Spread ¼ of filling over half of each rectangle and fold over to make a 6-inch square. Cut into 1½-inch squares (16 each).

4. Bake on ungreased cookie sheets at 300 degrees for 20 to 25 minutes or until just barely browned along bottom edges. Serve hot or cold.
Makes about 5 dozen.

*Apples are a member of the rose family.*

# NOTES

# APPLE ENTRÉES

Meat
Seafood
Poultry
Dairy

# APPLE CHEESE SOUFFLÉ

3 medium apples
1 medium onion
4 tablespoons butter
1 clove garlic, crushed, or ¼ teaspoon powdered garlic
¼ teaspoon each thyme, marjoram, and pepper
¼ cup flour
1 teaspoon salt
1 cup warm milk
1 tablespoon sherry (optional)
1 cup grated Cheddar cheese
¼ cup walnuts, finely chopped
4 egg yolks
6 egg whites
¼ teaspoon cream of tartar

1. Preheat oven to 375 degrees. Dice the apples and onion into fine pieces. Sauté in butter with the garlic and spices until soft. Stir in the flour and salt and cook over low heat for a few minutes. Add the milk and sherry. Beat with a wire whisk until the sauce is creamy and smooth. Remove from heat. Add cheese and walnuts.

2. Prepare a 6-cup soufflé dish or a deep casserole dish by buttering it and lightly dusting it with bread crumbs or flour. Beat egg yolks and add to the mixture. Beat the egg whites and cream of tartar until stiff but not dry. Fold into mixture.

3. Pour into prepared dish. Reduce oven temperature to 350 degrees. Bake 45 to 50 minutes. Serve immediately. Makes 4 to 6 servings.

# CHICKEN APPLE AMANDINE

**6 chicken breasts**
**8 tablespoons butter**
**2 tablespoons vegetable oil**
**Salt and pepper, to taste**
**3 tablespoons chopped scallions**
**4 large apples, peeled and cubed**
**1½ cups medium cream**
**3 tablespoons sliced roasted almonds**

1. Brown chicken breasts in 4 tablespoons butter and 2 tablespoons oil.

2. Add salt, pepper, and scallions and simmer about ½ hour.

3. Meanwhile, in separate skillet melt 4 tablespoons butter; add apples and cook about 10 minutes.

4. When chicken is cooked through and tender, add apples and cream and cook a few more minutes. Sprinkle with almonds and serve with rice, if desired. Makes 6 servings.

*But when I undress me*
*Each night upon my knees*
*Will ask the Lord to bless me*
*With apple pie and cheese!*
Eugene Field
*Apple Pie and Cheese*

# APPLE DOLMAS

½ cup chopped onion
1 tablespoon butter
1 cup beef or chicken bouillon
½ cup regular rice
½ cup grapenuts
2 teaspoons dried basil
¼ cup chopped parsley or 2 tablespoons dried parsley
1 pound ground beef
1½ teaspoons salt
Scant ¼ teaspoon black pepper
12 small or medium apples
Yogurt for sauce (optional)

1. Soften onion in butter over low heat. Add
   bouillon (1 cup water and bouillon cube) and
   bring to a boil. Add rice; cover, reduce heat to
   low. Cook 15 minutes or until water is absorbed.

2. Remove from heat; add grapenuts, basil, and
   parsley. Mix well and let stand 10 minutes,
   covered.

3. Add rice mixture to beef, salt, and pepper;
   mix well.

4. Cut apples in about 8 equal segments to about
   ½ inch from bottom; remove cores. (There is an
   apple "slicer-corer" on the market that will do
   this easily.)

5. Open apples slightly and stuff center cavity with
   meat-rice filling. Push filling in between slices
   and squeeze apple around filling. Any leftover

filling may be shaped into mini-sized balls and arranged over and between apples.

6. Place in 9 x 13-inch baking dish; add water to depth of ½ inch. Cover and bake at 350 degrees 30 minutes or until apples are soft but not mushy. Delicious served with yogurt as a sauce. May be served the next day. Makes 12.

# APPLES ON ENGLISH

**English muffins**
**Butter**
**Sliced cheese (American or Vermont Cheddar)**
**Sliced apple rings (fresh apples, peeled, cored, and**
   **sliced crosswise)**
**Bacon**

1. Toast English muffins and then butter.

2. Place cheese, then apple on muffin.

3. Sprinkle with dash of cinnamon.

4. Top with 2 slices of bacon per muffin.

5. Broil until bacon is cooked. (Bacon may be par-broiled first if desired.)

6. Good for brunch or light supper.

# APPLE AND SAUSAGE QUICHE

1¼ cups chopped apples
1 tablespoon lemon juice
1 tablespoon sugar
1 small onion, chopped
3 tablespoons butter
6 pork link sausages
4 eggs
1 pint sour cream (2 cups)
⅛ teaspoon nutmeg
Salt and pepper
9-inch pie shell*
1 cup grated Cheddar or Swiss cheese

1. Sprinkle apples with lemon juice, and then sugar; sauté with onion in butter until soft, but not mushy. Remove from heat and let cool for 20 minutes. In the meantime, cook sausages and set aside to cool.

2. Beat eggs well, and then blend in sour cream. Add nutmeg and salt and pepper to taste. Add apple mixture and pour into pie shell. Sausages may be cut in small pieces and combined with filling, or arranged on top in pinwheel fashion.

3. Bake in 350 degree oven for 45 to 60 minutes, or until knife inserted in filling comes out clean. Sprinkle with grated cheese about halfway through baking.

4. Let cool 5 minutes, then cut in wedges.
   Makes 1 quiche, about 8 servings.

   *Baked at 400 degrees for about 8 minutes.

# APPLE PANCAKE

2½ tablespoons flour
¼ teaspoon salt
½ cup milk
2 eggs, beaten
4 teaspoons sugar
Grated rind of 1 lemon
2 apples, peeled and thinly sliced
3 tablespoons butter
Confectioners' sugar (optional)

1. Combine flour, salt, and milk in mixing bowl and mix to a thin, smooth batter. Add the eggs, sugar, and lemon rind; beat well. Add apples; stir into batter.

2. Melt butter in 8-inch frying pan. Pour mixture into pan and distribute apples evenly over bottom. Cook over medium heat until set and golden brown on the underside.

3. Invert onto plate the same size as pan. Add a little more butter if needed to pan and slide back in to brown other side.

4. Turn onto heated serving dish; sprinkle with sifted confectioners' sugar if desired and serve hot. Makes 2 to 4 servings.

*Note:* The addition of the sugar makes this a dessert.

*Apples are the last fruit to be harvested in the fall.*

# APPLE AND KNOCKWURST SUPPER

**4 links knockwurst**
**2 medium onions, chopped**
**3 teaspoons margarine or butter**
**3 apples, peeled and chopped**
**½ cup chicken stock**
**½ teaspoon cinnamon**
**3 tablespoons brown sugar**
**Salt and pepper, to taste**

1. Boil knockwurst in water 10 minutes. Drain and set aside.

2. Sauté onions in margarine till just transparent. Add knockwurst and fry, covered, 10 minutes.

3. Add apples, chicken stock, cinnamon, sugar, salt, and pepper. Simmer 15 minutes. Serve with salad and baked potatoes, if desired.
   Makes 2 servings.

*The finished man of the world must eat of every*
*apple once.*
Ralph Waldo Emerson, *The Conduct of Life*

# BAKED CHICKEN BARBECUE

8 chicken breasts (or legs, or 4 of each)
Salt and pepper, to taste
½ cup melted butter or margarine
1½ cups chili sauce
⅓ cup water
2 medium onions, sliced
⅓ cup brown sugar, firmly packed
½ cup raisins
2 teaspoons Worcestershire sauce
6 apples, peeled and sliced

1. Rub chicken with salt and pepper. Brush with butter and broil lightly on both sides.

2. Combine chili sauce, water, onions, sugar, raisins, and Worcestershire sauce. Pour over chicken in shallow baking pan; cover with foil.

3. Bake at 325 degrees about 50 minutes, till chicken is cooked through. Add apples the last ½ hour of baking time. Makes 6 to 8 servings.

*Note:* This dish can be prepared in advance and refrigerated. Add apples when reheating.

*Thirty-five states provide the right conditions to grow apples commercially.*

# CHEESY-APPLE CRÊPES

*Crêpes:*
1 ¼ cups flour
3 eggs
1 ½ cups milk
¼ cup sugar
1 ½ teaspoons cinnamon
2 tablespoons butter
Pinch of salt

*Filling:*
½ cup sour cream
½ cup grated sharp Cheddar cheese
1 pound tart apples, peeled, cored, and chopped finely
Sugar to taste
Grated sharp Cheddar cheese for topping (about ½ cup)
Butter to cook crêpes

1. Crêpes: Combine ingredients in bowl. Beat with mixer until well blended. Let batter stand for at least 1 hour in refrigerator.

2. Filling: Combine sour cream and cheese; mix well. Stir in apples. Sweeten with sugar to taste.

3. Grease 6-inch skillet with butter. Place on medium heat. When water sprinkled on surface sizzles, the pan is ready. Pour ¼ cup of crêpe batter into pan; tilt until entire surface is covered. Return to heat. When batter no longer bubbles, place about ⅓ cup of filling in center. Fold sides over filling.

4. Remove from pan and place on baking sheet.

Repeat with remaining batter and filling.

5. Sprinkle grated cheese over each crêpe. Bake at 325 degrees until cheese melts.
Makes about 20 crêpes.

*Note:* Batter and filling store well, so individual crêpes can be made as needed; refrigerate unused batter and filling.

*"Very astonishing indeed! Strange thing!*
*(Turning the Dumpling round, rejoiced the King) . . .*
*"But, Goody, tell me where, where, where's the Seam?"*
*"Sire there's no Seam," Quoth she; "I never knew*
*That folks did Apple Dumplings sew."*
*"No!" cried the staring Monarch with a grin;*
*"How, how the devil got the Apple in?"*
John Wolcott,
*The Apple Dumplings and the King*

# CLARA'S CIDER CHICKEN

3 pounds chicken, cut up
2 tablespoons butter
¼ cup onions, chopped fine
¼ cup carrots, chopped fine
½ cup mushrooms, chopped fine
1 cup apples, chopped fine
1 tablespoon flour
Bouquet garni of 1 bay leaf, ½ teaspoon each parsley,
    thyme, and tarragon
1½ cups apple cider or apple juice
½ pint light cream

1. Brown chicken in butter in large, heavy pot.
   Chicken should be well browned.

2. Add vegetables, apples, and flour to chicken,
   also bouquet garni. Pour in cider. Cover
   and cook for 20 to 30 minutes, or until chicken
   is cooked through.

3. Remove chicken and add cream to liquid in pot;
   simmer until reduced and thickened. Return
   chicken to sauce to be sure it is hot; serve
   chicken pieces individually, or arrange on platter
   and pour sauce over all. Garnish with parsley,
   if desired. Makes about 6 servings.

*Use a metal measuring spoon (teaspoon size) as an apple
corer and baller. Cut the apple in half and use it to
remove the core.*

# CURRIED SHRIMP
# IN SEAFOOD SHELLS

3 tablespoons butter or margarine
1½ cups apples, peeled and diced
2 teaspoons curry powder
2 tablespoons flour
1¾ cups milk
1 teaspoon salt
½ teaspoon onion salt
Dash of nutmeg (optional)
2 cups shrimp, peeled and deveined (cut up if large)
2 hard-cooked eggs, cut in large pieces
¼ cup butter or margarine, melted
¾ cup toasted fine bread crumbs
¼ cup butter or margarine, melted
¾ cup Italian seasoned bread crumbs

1. Melt 3 tablespoons butter in saucepan; add
   apples and cook over low heat until very tender,
   about 15 minutes. Sprinkle with curry powder
   and flour; cook and stir a few minutes. Add milk
   gradually, blending well. Add seasonings and
   continue cooking until apples soften to sauce
   texture and mixture thickens.

2. Add shrimp and eggs. Distribute mixture
   among 4 to 6 seafood shells or ramekins
   or in shallow baking dish. Stir melted butter and
   bread crumbs together so that all are buttery;
   sprinkle on top of shrimp mixture. Bake at
   350 degrees 15 to 20 minutes or until golden and
   piping hot. Serve with fresh mushrooms with rice
   and chives and salad, if desired.
   Makes 4 to 6 servings.

# McINTOSH COUNTRY MEAT LOAF

2 pounds hamburger
1 cup fresh bread crumbs
1 egg, beaten
1 large apple, peeled and shredded
⅓ cup finely chopped onion
⅓ cup finely chopped celery (optional)
¼ cup molasses
Salt and pepper, to taste
¼ cup milk (about)
1 large apple, cut in eighths
*Glaze:*
2 tablespoons ketchup
2 tablepoons molasses
1 teaspoon mustard

1.  Mix all ingredients for meat loaf except milk and cut apple; blend well. Slowly add enough milk to make mixture moist but not wet. Place in 9x5-inch loaf pan; top with apple pieces.

2.  Bake at 350 degrees 1 hour. Remove from oven and top with mixture of glaze ingredients. Bake 15 minutes more. Makes 1 meat loaf.

*Note:* The following sauce is excellent with this meat loaf. Combine 1 cup sour cream, 1 tablespoon horseradish, 1 apple, peeled and shredded, salt and pepper to taste; chill well.

*Improve the flavor of your cake (any cake) and make it even more moist by scraping a small apple into the batter.*

# APPLESAUCED PORK CHOPS

4 lean pork chops
¼ pound butter, melted
½ cup onions, diced
3 pieces toast, diced
3 apples, diced
1 can (1 lb.) applesauce
Dash nutmeg
3 pinches pepper
½ cup apple wine (or apple juice)

1. Place pork chops in roasting pan; cover with melted butter. Top with remaining ingredients.

2. Bake at 400 degrees for ½ hour. Reduce temperature to 300 degrees and bake another ½ hour. Makes 4 servings.

*Note:* Chops may be browned first, if desired. Homemade applesauce may also be used in place of canned.

*The apples on the other side of the wall are the sweetest.*
W.G. Benham *Proverbs*

# SEAFOOD APPLE CASSEROLE

6 apples, medium size
½ pound butter
½ pound shrimps
½ pound scallops
2 cloves fresh garlic, finely diced
1½ cups boiled rice
½ cup apple cider
Salt and pepper to taste
½ tablespoon paprika
3 sprigs fresh parsley

1.  Peel and dice apples. Sauté over medium heat in 4 tablespoons butter. When apples are cooked, puree them.

2.  Fry the shrimps, scallops, and garlic in 4 table-spoons butter for about 7 minutes over medium heat.

3.  Spread rice evenly in 9 x 13-inch baking pan. Spread apple puree evenly on top of rice with apple cider. Neatly arrange shrimps and scallops as well as butter used for cooking them. Salt and pepper to taste and sprinkle with paprika. Pour ¼ pound melted butter over all.

4.  Bake at 350 degrees for ½ hour. Garnish with parsley. Makes 4 servings.

*Note:* Onions may be added for additional taste when apples are being cooked. Fillet of sole may be used instead of shrimps and scallops. Lemon slices may be used as a garnish.

# SPICY BEANS AND BEEF BAKE

3 slices bacon
1 large onion, sliced
1 stalk celery, sliced
1 pound hamburger
1 can (10¾ oz.) cream of tomato soup
1 can (1 lb.) kidney beans, drained
1 tart apple, peeled and chopped
2 tablespoons brown sugar
Salt and pepper to taste
1 tart apple, sliced

1. Sauté bacon in large, heavy skillet until nearly crisp; remove and drain.

2. In bacon drippings, sauté onion and celery until soft and golden, but not brown. Add hamburger, broken up, and cook until browned, stirring often.

3. Remove from heat; add soup, beans, chopped apple, brown sugar, salt and pepper.

4. Place in 1½-quart casserole; arrange bacon strips and sliced apple on top. Bake at 350 degrees about 25 minutes. Serve with salad and cornbread, if desired, for tasty and economical dinner. Makes 5-6 servings.

*If browning occurs near the core of an apple, it indicates that the fruit has been stored at too low a temperature.*

# SUGAR AND SPICE POT ROAST

4 pounds beef shoulder pot roast
3 onions, diced
2 garlic cloves, minced
1 stalk celery, diced
1 carrot, diced
2 apples, peeled and diced
2 teaspoons salt
2 cups tomato juice
2 tablespoons brown sugar
10 gingersnaps

1. Heat a heavy pot and braise the meat until evenly browned on all sides.

2. Add remaining ingredients and simmer for about 1 ½ hours or until the meat is tender.
   Makes 6 to 8 servings.

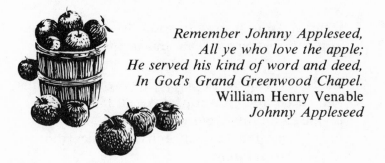

*Remember Johnny Appleseed,*
*All ye who love the apple;*
*He served his kind of word and deed,*
*In God's Grand Greenwood Chapel.*
William Henry Venable
*Johnny Appleseed*

# NOTES

# APPLE SIDE DISHES

Vegetables
Salads
Stuffings
Condiments

# BAKED STUFFED ACORN SQUASH

**3 acorn or Des Moines squash**
**3 medium apples**
**¾ cup nut meats (optional)**
**¼ cup melted butter or margarine**
**½ cup maple syrup or honey**

1. Cut squash in halves; scoop out seeds. Dice apples, but leave skins on; combine with nuts.

2. Divide apple-nut mixture among 6 squash halves; drizzle butter and syrup over each.

3. Place in baking pan; pour in hot water to ½ inch. Cover pan loosely with foil. Bake at 400 degrees for 45 minutes or until squash is tender.

   Makes 6 servings.

*Isaac Newton is said to have thought up the law of gravity sitting under an apple tree.*

# APPLE CIDER SALAD

**2 envelopes unflavored gelatin**
**3½ cups apple juice or cider**
**2 tablespoons sugar**
**Dash of salt**
**2 medium sized apples**
**½ cup chopped carrots**
**½ cup chopped celery**
**Lettuce and dressing as desired**

1. Combine gelatin with ½ cup apple juice, sugar, and salt in saucepan; stir over low heat until gelatin is dissolved. Add remaining apple juice and chill in refrigerator until partially set, but not firm.

2. Pour about 1 cup gelatin mixture into 6-cup mold. Arrange slices of 1 apple on top and cover with a layer of gelatin. Combine other apple, chopped, with carrots and celery; combine with remaining gelatin mixture and pour into mold. Chill until set.

3. Unmold and serve with lettuce and dressing as desired. Makes 8 or more servings.

*Apple trees need 30 to 60 days of chill weather to shed their leaves and take a winter siesta.*

# NEW ENGLAND AUTUMN CASSEROLE

2½ cups sliced pumpkin or winter squash,
  pared and seeded
1½ cups sliced apples
¼ cup butter, melted
3 to 4 tablespoons brown sugar
1 teaspoon cinnamon
½ cup walnuts or almonds, broken up
Salt to taste
Butter

1. Place a layer of pumpkin, then a layer of apples
   in a 2-quart casserole. (Pumpkin or squash will
   not cook as quickly, so slice more thinly
   than apples.)

2. Combine butter, sugar, cinnamon, nuts, and salt;
   drizzle some over apples and pumpkin. Continue
   alternating layers and drizzling with butter and
   sugar mixture till all ingredients have been used.
   Dot with a bit more butter.

3. Cover casserole and bake in 350 degree oven for
   45 to 60 minutes, until pumpkin and apples
   are tender. Makes 4 servings.

*Three cups of peeled and sliced apples equal about three
medium apples which is about one pound of apples.*

# SWEET APPLE CABBAGE

**1 pound red cabbage, shredded**
**2 cups chopped apples**
**⅓ cup melted margarine or butter**
**2 tablespoons sugar**
**2 teaspoons salt**
**1 teaspoon cinnamon**

1. In a large pot, toss together all ingredients. Cook over low heat, stirring occasionally, until tender, about 15 to 20 minutes. Add a little water during cooking, if necessary.

2. Serve immediately as side dish for pork, poultry, or beef. Makes about 8 servings.

*The United States produces approximately one-quarter of the world's apple crop.*

# SWEET POTATO SCALLOP

½ cup bread crumbs or crushed cornflakes
3 tablespoons butter, melted
⅓ cup brown sugar
1 teaspoon salt
¼ teaspoon cinnamon
¼ teaspoon nutmeg
1½ cups thinly sliced sweet potatoes
1½ cups chopped apples, peeled
1 teaspoon lemon juice
3 tablespoons water

1. Stir bread crumbs into butter; add sugar, salt, and spices. Place half the mixture in greased casserole. Add half the sweet potatoes, then half the apples.

2. Combine lemon juice with water; sprinkle half on apples and potatoes. Repeat layers, ending with the crumb mixture. Cover; bake at 350 degrees for 45 minutes.

3. Uncover and brown lightly.
   Makes 6 servings.

*An apple placed with a bag of potatoes helps prevent them from sprouting.*

# APPLE SOUFFLÉ SALAD

1 pkg. (3 oz.) lemon-flavored gelatin
1 cup boiling water
¾ cup cold water
3 tablespoons lemon juice
½ teaspoon salt
¼ cup mayonnaise
2 apples, peeled, cored, and diced
2 sticks celery, sliced
½ cup seeded grapes
¼ cup walnuts, chopped
Frosted grapes and apple slices (see below)

1. Dissolve gelatin in boiling water. Add cold water, lemon juice, salt, and mayonnaise; blend well with rotary beater. Pour into ice cube tray and chill in freezer 15 to 20 minutes.

2. Turn semi-frozen mixture into bowl and whip until light and fluffy. Fold in apples, celery, grapes, and walnuts; pour into 1-quart mold or individual molds. Chill until firm.

3. To prepare frosted grapes and apple slices, dip fruit in beaten egg white, roll in sugar and chill. Use as garnish for salad.
   Makes 6 servings.

*Apples were imported from England in 1629 by John Winthrop, Colonial Governor of Massachusetts.*

# APPLE YOGURT MOLDED SALAD

1 cup apple juice
1⅓ cups water
2 tablespoons gelatin
¼ cup sugar (or less)
2 cups chopped apples
2 tablespoons lemon juice
¼ teaspoon salt
½ cup chopped nuts (optional)
6 ounces apple yogurt

1. Combine apple juice and water in saucepan; sprinkle gelatin over and stir over low heat until dissolved.

2. Add sugar, apples, lemon juice, salt, and nuts. Chill in refrigerator until partially set.

3. Fold in yogurt and pour into mold and chill until firmly set. May be served as salad on lettuce leaves, or as dessert topped with whipped cream. Makes 8 servings.

*The fresh fruit color of apples can be retained by dipping the cut fruit into a mixture of citrus juice and water. Alternatively, a commercial ascorbic acid color keeper can be used. Cortlands will stay white longer than other varieties.*

# FESTIVE FRUIT SALAD BOWL

**6 medium apples, peeled, cored, and sliced**
**1 can (8¼ oz.) pineapple chunks, drained**
**2 bananas, sliced**
**½ cup finely chopped walnuts**
**½ bag (16 oz.) miniature marshmallows**
*Dressing:*
**1 cup mayonnaise**
**4 tablespoons milk**

1.  Mix fruit, nuts, and marshmallows in large bowl.

2.  Mix dressing ingredients well with egg beater
    or wire whisk. Toss with fruit mixture; chill.

3.  Serve on lettuce leaves, or plain as dessert.
    Makes about 8 servings.

*Brown sugar may be kept moist and thus soft by
including an apple in the container.*

# FROSTY APPLE SALAD

2 pkgs. (3 oz. each) cream cheese
1 can (8¾ oz.) crushed pineapple
2 tablespoons syrup from maraschino cherries
¼ cup chopped maraschino cherries
1½ cups chopped apples (with skins on)
½ cup dairy sour cream

1. Mix softened cream cheese, undrained pineapple, and cherry syrup. Blend in blender a few seconds, or cream well together with fork.

2. Add chopped cherries and apples; fold in sour cream. Freeze in ice cube tray until firm. Cut in squares and serve on lettuce.
Makes about 8 servings.

# JIFFY APPLE STUFFING

2 or 3 medium onions, chopped
2 stalks celery, diced
¼ pound butter or margarine
1 pkg. (8 oz.) herb bread stuffing
1 cup walnuts, coarsely chopped
4 apples, peeled and cut up

1. Sauté onions and celery in butter until
   light brown.

2. Prepare packaged stuffing as directed.

3. Add onions, celery, walnuts, and apples.
   (Macs are good.) Makes stuffing for 6 to 8
   pounds of poultry.

*The Hebrew word for apple does not appear in the
Biblical account of Adam and Eve. Since it's doubtful
that the apple existed in that part of the world at that time
it is believed that the forbidden fruit may have been
the apricot which was plentiful in the Holy Land.*

# APPLE JELLY

3 pounds apples*
3 cups water
3 cups sugar
2 tablespoons lemon juice, or
½ teaspoon peppermint extract (both optional)

1. Remove stem and blossom ends of apples, but do not core or peel. Cut apples into small chunks and put in kettle with water. Cover and bring to boil over high heat; lower heat and simmer until apples are very tender, about 20 minutes.

2. Turn cooked fruit and juice into jelly bag or several thicknesses of dampened cheesecloth; let juice drain into kettle, shifting pulp occasionally to keep juice flowing.

3. Combine 4 cups of the apple juice in kettle with sugar and lemon juice, if desired. Boil rapidly until mixture is 8 degrees F. above the boiling point of water, or until jelly sheets from a spoon.

4. Skim foam off jelly and pour immediately into hot jars. Seal. Makes about 4 half pints.

*Use slightly underripe apples, or at least one-fourth underripe and three-fourths ripe.

# TOMATO CHUTNEY

**4 pounds ripe tomatoes, cored and chopped**
**1 pound apples, cored, peeled, and chopped**
**3 onions, minced**
**2 cups vinegar**
**2 tablespoons salt**
**2 cups packed brown sugar**
**1 cup seeded raisins**
**1 teaspoon dry mustard**
**½ teaspoon cayenne pepper**

1. Mix all ingredients and cook, stirring occasionally, 1½ hours, or until thick and clear.

2. Pour into hot sterilized jars and seal. Process in boiling water bath for 10 minutes.
   Makes about 5 pints.

*Apple: the earth, the globe; any large town or city. A street or district in which excitement or activity may be found.*

# VERMONT APPLE BUTTER

**4 pounds apples**
**2 cups sugar**
**1 teaspoon grated lemon peel**
**¼ teaspoon salt**
**¼ teaspoon cinnamon**
**¼ teaspoon cloves**
**¼ teaspoon allspice**
**⅛ teaspoon nutmeg (optional)**

1. Core apples and cut in eighths. Cook with about ½ cup water or cider until tender and mushy, about 45 minutes, over low heat.

2. Put apples through a colander or food mill. Add sugar, lemon peel, salt, and spices; cook until thick and glossy, stirring frequently, about 30 minutes.

3. Pour into hot sterilized jars. Seal. Process in boiling water bath 10 minutes.
   Makes 4 half pints.

# INDIAN RELISH

**12 green tomatoes**
**12 tart apples, peeled and cored**
**3 onions, peeled**
**5 cups white vinegar**
**5 cups sugar**
**1 teaspoon red pepper**
**3 teaspoons ginger**
**1 teaspoon turmeric**
**1 teaspoon salt**

1. Chop or slice thin the green tomatoes. Slice or chop apples. Chop onions. Transfer to a large strainer or colander and drain off about 2 cups liquid. Discard the liquid.

2. Meanwhile, heat the vinegar, sugar, spices, and salt together in large saucepan. Cook until liquid boils vigorously. Remove from stove, add the chopped mixture. Cook again to active boil. Reduce heat and cook slowly for ten minutes, stirring frequently.

3. Pack the relish in sterilized jars. Seal. Process in boiling water bath 10 minutes.
   Makes about 4 quarts or 8 pints.

*He kept him as the apple of his eye.*
The Bible, *I Samuel, Deuteronomy*

# ROSEY APPLESAUCE

5 to 6 pounds apples
  (about 15 or 20 medium size)
1 cup water
1 cup granulated sugar
½ cup light brown sugar
1 teaspoon cinnamon (optional)

1. Wash apples. Do not peel or core. Remove only bud and stem areas.

2. Quarter apples and place in 5 quart pan with 1 cup water.

3. Bring to boil and simmer 30 to 40 minutes until the pulp softens and separates from the peel. Stir occasionally.

4. Press through a food mill or sieve or colander.

5. Add sugar and cinnamon, if desired, to warm applesauce and allow to stand until cool enough to eat. Serve warm or chilled.
   Makes 6-8 cups thick, rosey colored applesauce.

*The first apples grown in the United States were probably obtained from trees planted in Boston, Massachusetts, from which "the fair pippins" were plucked on October 16, 1639.*

# NOTES

# APPLE BREADS & PASTRIES

Yeast Breads
Coffee Cakes
Doughnuts & Muffins
Strudels

# APPLE HONEY BUNS

½ cup butter
1 cup firmly packed brown sugar
1 teaspoon cinnamon
1 tablespoon honey
⅓ cup milk
1 pkg. (13¾ oz.) hot roll mix
¾ cup very warm water
⅓ cup sugar
1 egg
½ cup chopped nuts
1½ cups chopped apples

1. Combine butter, brown sugar, cinnamon, honey, and milk in small saucepan. Stir over low heat until butter melts and mixture is smooth. Pour half into ungreased 13 x 9 x 2-inch baking pan; reserve remaining mixture.

2. Dissolve yeast from hot roll mix in warm water in large bowl; stir in sugar, egg, and nuts. Add flour mixture and apples; blend well.

3. Drop dough by heaping tablespoonfuls on top of brown sugar mixture in pan, forming 15 rolls. Drizzle with remaining brown sugar mixture.

4. Cover; let rise in warm place until light and doubled in bulk, 45 to 60 minutes.

5. Preheat oven to 350 degrees; bake 30 to 35 minutes or until golden. Let stand a few minutes; remove from pan. Makes 15 rolls.

# SWEET APPLE BREAD

2 loaves frozen bread dough
2 tablespoons butter or margarine
2 cups diced apples
¾ cup light brown sugar
2 teaspoons cinnamon
½ cup raisins
*Glaze:*
1½ cups sifted confectioners' sugar
2 tablespoons milk
½ teaspoon lemon juice
¼ teaspoon cinnamon (optional)
½ cup chopped nuts for garnish

1. Place bread dough in lightly greased large bowl; let rise until doubled in size.

2. Roll out dough to about ½ inch thickness, in rectangular shape. Spread with butter; sprinkle with apples, brown sugar, cinnamon, and raisins.

3. Roll up like jelly roll; place seam side down in large (10-inch) tube pan. Wet the two ends of roll with water and pinch together to seal.

4. Let rise in a warm place until doubled in size. Bake in 375 degree oven about 35 minutes or until golden brown. Cool on cake rack.

5. Glaze: Blend confectioners' sugar, milk, lemon juice, and cinnamon together until smooth. Remove bread from pan and spread with glaze. Sprinkle with nuts.
   Makes 1 bread ring.

# APPLE RAISIN BRAID

1 pkg. dry yeast
¼ cup warm water
¼ cup sugar
½ cup milk
¼ cup margarine or butter
1 egg
1 cup grated apples
3 cups flour
½ teaspoon salt
*Filling:*
½ cup sugar
2 tablespoons flour
½ cup water
1 tablespoon lemon juice
1½ cups raisins
2 cups chopped apples
*Icing:* **(recipe follows)**

1. Filling: Mix sugar and flour, add water and lemon juice; mix in raisins. Heat until thick and raisins are soft. Add apples.

2. Mix yeast in warm water; add sugar. Scald milk; add margarine. Add milk mixture and egg to yeast; stir in apples, flour, and salt. Knead until well blended; let rise until doubled.

3. Knead again; divide dough into two parts. Roll or flatten to about ½ inch thickness on lightly greased cookie sheet. At 1-inch intervals along sides, slit dough ⅓ of the width, leaving the center uncut. Spread center with ½ of filling.

4. Braid by bringing side strips over filling,

alternating sides, crossing them in the middle. Repeat with other half of dough. Let rise until doubled.

5. Bake in 375 degree oven for 30 minutes or until golden brown.

6. Icing: Combine 1 tablespoon melted margarine or butter and 1 tablespoon milk; add confectioners' sugar until spreading consistency. Use as glaze for top of bread. Makes 2 braids.

*Stay me with flagons,*
*Comfort me with apples;*
*For I am sick with love.*
The Bible, *The Song of Solomon*

# APPLE CHEESE BREAD

½ cup butter
⅓ cup sugar
⅓ cup honey
2 eggs
1 cup whole wheat flour
1 cup unbleached white flour
1 teaspoon baking powder
½ teaspoon baking soda
½ teaspoon salt
1½ cups shredded apples
½ cup shredded sharp Cheddar cheese
½ cup chopped walnuts

1. Cream butter and sugar. Mix in honey and eggs. Sift together dry ingredients and add to creamed mixture. Fold in apples, cheese, and nuts.

2. Spoon batter into a greased 9 x 5-inch loaf pan. Bake at 350 degrees for 50 to 60 minutes. Remove from pan and cool thoroughly. Tastes best the next day. Makes 1 loaf.

# APPLE COFFEE CAKE
## prepared the day before

⅓ cup margarine or butter
1 cup sugar
2 eggs
1 teaspoon vanilla
1½ cups flour
2 teaspoons baking powder
½ teaspoon nutmeg
¼ teaspoon salt
⅔ cup milk
4 apples, pared and finely chopped
1 tablespoon cinnamon
1 tablespoon sugar
½ cup chopped walnuts

1. Stir margarine to soften, add sugar and cream until fluffy. Add eggs and vanilla; beat well. Sift together dry ingredients. Add to creamed mixture alternately with milk, beating smooth after each addition. Fold in apples. Pour into greased 9-inch square pan.

2. Combine remaining ingredients, sprinkle over batter. Bake in 375 degree oven 25 to 30 minutes. Makes 1 coffee cake.

*Note:* This cake may be prepared the night before and kept in refrigerator until ready to bake.

> *He that is won with a nut, may be*
> *lost with an apple.*
> Thomas Fuller, *Gnomologia I*

# BUTTERY APPLE FLAKE LOAF

⅓ cup butter
4 apples, peeled and diced
½ teaspoon cinnamon
1 cup crushed macaroon cookies
2 pkgs. (8 oz. each) refrigerated Quick Butterflake
  Dinner Rolls
3 tablespoons coarse crystal sugar

1. Melt 4 tablespoons of the butter in skillet; add apples and cinnamon, turning frequently, until golden. Fold in crumbs, mixing well.

2. Halve rolls; spoon in 1 tablespoon apple mixture; put together. Stand rolls on edge in lightly buttered 9 x 5 x 3-inch glass loaf dish, making 2 rows.

3. Spoon remaining filling in between rolls. Drizzle loaf with remaining butter, melted. Sprinkle with coarse sugar.

4. Bake in 350 degree oven 30 to 35 minutes. Loosen edges, turn out of dish immediately. Serve warm. Makes 1 loaf.

*Note:* Sugar cubes may be crushed for coarse crystal sugar.

*About the only part of the apple growing that hasn't changed through the ages is the apple-picking . . . and that hasn't changed since Adam and Eve.*
John N. Ravage, *Vermont Life*

# APPLE PASTRY LOGS

*Pastry:*
½ cup margarine or butter
1 cup sifted flour
1 egg yolk, beaten
¼ cup sour cream
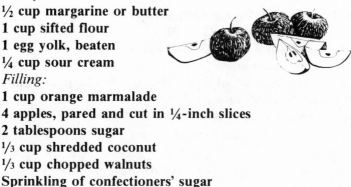
*Filling:*
1 cup orange marmalade
4 apples, pared and cut in ¼-inch slices
2 tablespoons sugar
⅓ cup shredded coconut
⅓ cup chopped walnuts
Sprinkling of confectioners' sugar

1. Cut margarine into flour until mixture resembles small crumbs. Combine egg yolk and sour cream; mix with flour until dough forms a ball. Split dough in half; chill at least 3 hours or overnight.

2. Roll each ball of dough into rectangle, about 12 by 9 inches.

3. Divide filling ingredients in half for each log. Spread marmalade along long edge of dough rectangle. Lay 2 or 3 layers of apples in single row on marmalade. Sprinkle with sugar, then sprinkle with coconut and nuts.

4. Lift pastry near filling side and roll. Place on lightly greased baking sheet, seam side down, moisten with milk to seal, tucking ends under.

5. Bake at 350 degrees for about 25 minutes or until browned. Juices will probably run, so remove gently from pan. Sprinkle with confectioners' sugar. Serve warm. May be reheated. Makes 2 logs.

# APPLE NAPOLEONS

**10-ounce pkg. frozen patty shells (6)**
**2 cups grated apples (2 to 3)**
**1½ cups sifted confectioners' sugar**
**¼ teaspoon nutmeg**
**1 cup refrigerated whipped topping or whipped cream**
**½ cup chopped walnuts**
**3 to 4 teaspoons milk**
**½ teaspoon almond extract**

1. Thaw patty shells to room temperature. Place
   3 patty shells on floured board, place the
   remaining 3 shells on top of them. Roll out
   to form a rectangle 12 x 8 inches. Cut into 8
   3 x 4-inch rectangles. Bake on an ungreased
   baking sheet in 400 degree oven 50 to 20 minutes
   until golden brown. Cool.

2. While pastry is baking, grate apples. Add ½ cup
   of the sugar, nutmeg, whipped topping, and nuts
   to apples. Split cooled rectangles in half length-
   wise. Place apple mixture on bottom half, cover
   with top half.

3. Combine 1 cup sugar with milk and almond
   extract. Spoon over top of each napoleon.
   Makes 8 servings.

# BAKED APPLE COCONUT DOUGHNUTS

2½ cups sifted flour
2½ teaspoons baking powder
½ teaspoon salt
½ teaspoon nutmeg
½ cup sugar
⅔ cup shortening
1 cup milk
1 egg, well beaten
1 cup grated apple
½ cup shredded coconut
⅓ cup butter or margarine, melted
⅓ cup sugar
1 teaspoon cinnamon

1. Sift together flour, baking powder, salt, nutmeg, and sugar. Cut in the shortening until mixture is fine.

2. Mix together milk, egg, apple, and coconut; add all at once to flour mixture and mix quickly and thoroughly.

3. Fill greased large size muffin tins two-thirds full. Bake in 350 degree oven for 25 minutes or until golden brown.

4. Remove from pan. Immediately dunk doughnut tops in melted butter and then in combined sugar and cinnamon mixture.
Makes about 18 doughnuts.

*Unripe or hard apples should be held at a cool 60°-70° F. room temperature until ready to eat.*

# OLD-FASHIONED APPLE
# DOUGHNUT BALLS

2 eggs
1 cup sugar
1 teaspoon salt
1 teaspoon nutmeg
½ teaspoon cinnamon
¼ cup soft shortening
1 cup buttermilk
3¾ cups flour
1 teaspoon baking powder
1 teaspoon baking soda
1 cup grated apple
Fat for deep frying
Cinnamon and sugar

1. Beat eggs, sugar, salt, spices, and shortening well. Add buttermilk.

2. Combine dry ingredients, stir into batter; add 1 cup grated apple (1 or 2 according to size). Let set in refrigerator while fat heats.

3. Heat fat to about 370 degrees. Drop batter by teaspoonfuls into hot fat, turning once. Roll doughnut balls in a mixture of cinnamon and sugar while still slightly warm.
   Makes 5 dozen doughnut balls.

*Controlled Atmosphere Storage (CA Storage) allows apples to be eaten year-round. The process slows down the rate of respiration and the apple continues to "live" up to ten months.*

# MINI-APPLE STRUDELS

2 apples, pared, cored, and sliced
½ teaspoon cinnamon
2 teaspoons sugar
½ cup walnuts, chopped
¼ cup dark brown sugar
½ cup flour
¼ teaspoon cinnamon
¼ cup margarine or butter, softened
3-ounce pkg. cream cheese, softened
8-ounce pkg. Crescent Dinner Rolls

1. Preheat oven to 375 degrees and grease a
   baking sheet.

2. In a small bowl, place sliced apples and chop fine.
   Add cinnamon, sugar, and walnuts; blend well.
   Set aside.

3. In another bowl, combine brown sugar, flour,
   cinnamon, and soft margarine; mix until crumbly,
   set aside. In a small dish, soften cream cheese,
   set aside.

4. Separate crescents into 8 triangles. On each
   triangle spread softened cream cheese, spoon a
   heaping tablespoon apple mixture over that, then
   roll very carefully into a crescent shape as
   directed on the can, tucking ends under.

5. Sprinkle with brown sugar mixture. Place on
   greased baking sheet with tucked ends on underside. Repeat until all 8 are made.

6. Bake for 10 to 12 mintues. Serve hot or cold.
   Makes 8.

# VIENNESE APPLE STRUDEL

1 cup butter or margarine
3 cups sifted flour
½ cup confectioners' sugar
2 eggs, separated
6 tablespoons milk
½ cup buttered bread crumbs
4 cups thinly sliced apples
¼ cup honey
4 sugar lumps, coarsely crushed
¼ cup plumped golden raisins
¼ cup finely slivered almonds
1 teaspoon grated orange rind
1 tablespoon orange juice
Whipped cream in pastry tube
Maraschino cherries for garnish

1. Cut butter finely into combined flour and sugar.
   Combine egg yolks and milk; stir
   gradually into mixture; form dough into a ball.
   Roll out to a 17 x 13-inch rectangle. Sprinkle
   buttered crumbs over dough; arrange slightly
   overlapping apple slices over center of rectangle.

2. Combine honey, sugar, raisins, almonds, orange
   rind, and juice; spoon over apples, pressing down
   gently. Draw one side of dough over filling; top
   with remaining side. Seal edges.

3. Arrange strudel on baking sheet; brush top with
   slightly beaten egg white. Bake in a 350 degree
   oven for 45 minutes or until flaky and golden.

4. Press ruffles of cream in 4 rows. Garnish cream

with chopped cherries and whole cherries
as desired.
Makes 16 servings.

# APPLE MUFFINS

¾ cup milk
1 egg, beaten
¼ cup melted butter or margarine
2 cups unsifted flour
½ cup sugar
1 tablespoon baking powder
½ teaspoon salt
1 teaspoon cinnamon (optional)
1 cup finely chopped apples
½ cup raisins

1. Add milk to egg; stir in fat. Mix dry ingredients
   thoroughly; stir in apples and raisins.

2. Add liquid mixture and stir just until most of the
   dry ingredients are moistened. Do not overmix;
   batter should be lumpy.

3. Fill greased muffin tins two-thirds full. Bake at
   400 degrees 20 to 25 minutes until golden brown.
   Makes 12 muffins.

# RAISIN SPICE OATMEAL BREAD

1½ cups sifted all-purpose flour
1 teaspoon baking powder
1 teaspoon baking soda
1½ teaspoons salt
1 teaspoon cinnamon
½ teaspoon nutmeg
⅔ cup firmly packed brown sugar
2 eggs, beaten
1 cup sweetened applesauce
1 cup quick or old-fashioned oats, uncooked
1 cup raisins
⅓ cup vegetable oil or melted shortening

1. Sift together flour, baking powder, soda, salt, and spices. Add sugar, eggs, and applesauce; beat until well blended. Stir in oats, raisins, and oil.

2. Fill a greased 9 x 5-inch loaf pan. Bake at 350 degrees about 1 hour.

3. Remove from pan immediately; cool. For ease in slicing, wrap cooled bread and store one day. Makes 1 loaf.

*Late maturing apples picked after the first frost are juicier, crispier, and contain more fruit sugar.*

# APPLE PIES, CAKES, & TORTES

# APPLE CHEESE PIE

¾ cup sugar
2 tablespoons flour
¼ teaspoon salt
1 cup small curd cottage cheese
2 eggs
1 tablespoon lemon juice
1 teaspoon vanilla
2½ cups chopped apples
9-inch pie shell (graham cracker or pastry)
⅓ cup flour
¼ cup sugar
1 teaspoon cinnamon
4 tablespoons butter

1. Combine ¾ cup sugar, 2 tablespoons flour, and salt. Blend in cottage cheese, eggs, lemon juice, and vanilla; mix thoroughly. Stir in apples. Spoon into pie shell.

2. Sift together remaining flour, sugar, and cinnamon. Cut in butter until mixture is crumbly; sprinkle over pie. Bake in 375 degree oven for 40 to 50 minutes.
   Makes 1 pie.

*Apple pie without cheese*
*Is like a kiss without a squeeze.*
Unknown

# APPLE CHEESE TARTS

3-ounce pkg. cream cheese
1 tablespoon apple cider
½ cup heavy cream
2 tablespoons confectioners' sugar
1 roll (1 lb. 2 oz.) refrigerated Sugar Slice'n Bake Cookies
3 medium sized apples, thinly sliced

1. Combine softened cream cheese and apple cider. Whip cream and sugar until stiff; fold into cream cheese.

2. Bake cookies as directed on package. After removing from oven, immediately press the center of each cookie with a tablespoon to form a well. Remove from baking sheet; cool.

3. Place apple slices in boiling water for 1 minute. Rinse with cold water.

4. Just before serving, place about 1 teaspoon of filling on each cookie. Top each with two apple slices. Makes 3½ dozen tarts.

*Apples contain vitamins A, C, thiamine, and riboflavin. They are also a supplemental source for such minerals as calcium, phosphorus, and iron.*

# BARNEY'S HOT APPLE PIE

1½ lbs. peeled and sliced apples
1 cup raisins
1 cup sugar
¾ cup white wine
1 tablespoon cinnamon
1 teaspoon nutmeg
20 slices thin sliced white bread
¾ cup butter, melted
5 Duralex glass bowls (5-inch diameter) or
   5 Pyrex 10-oz. deep pie dishes
   (shaped like custard cups only larger)

1. Combine apples, raisins, sugar, wine, cinnamon, and nutmeg. Cook over medium heat for 5 minutes. Stir gently so as not to break apple slices.

2. Trim crusts off bread slices. Cut corners off 10 slices to form each into octagon shape. Cut each of remaining 10 slices into 4 squares.

3. Grease inside of each bowl with melted butter. Dip one face of each octagon in melted butter and place buttered side down in bottom of each dish.

4. Dip corners of bread squares in butter and fit into each bowl as follows: squeeze point of 1 square into octagon on bottom, therefore, covering side of bowl; repeat with 7 more squares over-lapping around bowl, thus completely encircling bowl. (You will use 8 squares per bowl.)

5. Fill each bowl with apple mixture. Completely soak remaining 5 octagons in butter and place

one on top of each bowl, completely sealing in ingredients.

6. Place bowls on a baking sheet and bake in preheated 350 degree oven for 45 minutes or until golden brown on sides as well as top.

7. Remove from oven and allow to stand for about 10 minutes.

8. Invert bowl in center of dinner plate. Remove bowl and encircle pie with your favorite vanilla sauce or rum sauce.
Makes 5 pies.

*To accelerate the ripeness of apples, keep them in a crisper for a few days and then let them sit outside till ripe enough.*

# APPLE CUSTARD CREAM PIE

9-inch pie shell, fluted high, unbaked
1 tablespoon flour
8 medium sized apples, quartered
1 cup sugar
1 teaspoon cinnamon
Dash of nutmeg
1 tablespoon butter
*Custard topping:*
1 small egg
½ cup light cream
¼ cup sugar
1 teaspoon vanilla

1. Dust bottom of pie shell with flour. Arrange apples in pie shell; sprinkle with sugar combined with spices. Dot with butter.

2. Cover tightly with foil and bake at 425 degrees about ½ hour, until apples are cooked through.

3. Meanwhile, combine ingredients for custard topping and beat well. Pour evenly over apples in pie shell.

4. Lower oven temperature to 325 degrees and bake for 35 minutes longer.
   Makes 1 pie.

# APPLE PRALINE PIE

5 cups apples, peeled and sliced
½ cup sugar
2 tablespoons quick cooking tapioca
1½ teaspoons lemon juice
½ cup flour
¼ cup dark brown sugar
½ cup pecans, chopped
¼ cup butter
9-inch pie shell, unbaked

1. Combine apples, sugar, tapioca, and lemon juice in large bowl; let stand 15 minutes.

2. Combine remaining ingredients, cutting in butter until crumbs form.

3. Sprinkle one-third crumb mixture in bottom of pie shell. Cover with apple mixture; sprinkle remaining crumbs on top.

4. Bake at 450 degrees for 10 minutes. Reduce heat to 350 degrees and continue baking about 25 minutes until nicely browned.
   Makes 1 pie.

*Apple pie was part of English cookery at least two centuries before the settling of America. The English version is made with puff paste.*

# APPLE FLAN

*Pastry:*
**2 cups flour**
**½ cup butter or margarine**
**¼ cup super fine sugar**
**2 egg yolks**
**¼ teaspoon vanilla**
**¼ cup water**

1. Sift flour into a mixing bowl, make a well; add butter, cut in small pieces, sugar, egg yolks, vanilla, and water. Blend with fingertips. Knead lightly. Chill for 30 minutes.

2. Roll out to line an 8-inch flan ring or shallow cake pan. Fill with filling.

*Filling:*
**2 pounds cooking apples**
**⅝ cup white wine or apple juice**
**Grated rind of ½ lemon**
**4 tablespoons butter**
**½ cup granulated sugar**
**4 crisp apples**
**¼ cup apricot jam**
**1 tablespoon prune juice or water**

1. Peel and core cooking apples, cut into large slices. Place apples in saucepan with wine or apple juice, lemon rind, butter, and ¼ cup sugar. Cover, simmer gently until apples are tender.

2. Puree cooked apples in blender, place in unbaked pie shell.

3. Peel and core 4 remaining apples, slice thinly, arrange overlapping on top of puree. Sprinkle with remaining ¼ cup sugar. Bake at 375 degrees for 25 to 30 minutes until golden brown.

4. Heat apricot jam with prune juice. Spoon over hot cooked flan. Serve with whipped cream if desired.

*The apple's reputation of being nature's "toothbrush" comes from the evidence that eating raw apples "brushes" the teeth, cleanses the mouth of 96.7% of oral bacteria and exercises the teeth and gums. Dentists recommend that the best times to eat an apple are after meals and just before going to bed.*

# CARAMEL APPLE PIE

5½ cups apples, pared and sliced
¼ cup water
9-inch pie shell, unbaked
¾ cup graham cracker crumbs
¾ cup sugar
1 tablespoon flour
½ teaspoon cinnamon
½ teaspoon nutmeg
¼ teaspoon salt
½ cup pecans, chopped
⅓ cup butter or margarine, melted
½ lb. caramels
½ cup hot milk

1. Cook apple slices in water 3 minutes. Cool.

2. Arrange apple slices in pie shell. Mix crumbs, sugar, flour, cinnamon, nutmeg, salt, pecans, and melted butter. Sprinkle over apples.

3. Bake at 425 degrees 10 minutes; reduce heat to 350 degrees and continue baking 20 minutes.

4. Meanwhile, combine caramels and milk in top of double boiler; cook over hot water until smooth.

5. Pour caramel sauce over top of hot pie. Reduce heat to 250 degrees and continue baking 10 minutes. Makes 1 pie.

*Note:* Pie will slice best if allowed to cool until caramel has set slightly.

# CRANBERRY GLAZED APPLE CREAM CHEESE PIE

*Crumb crust:*
1½ cups graham cracker or cookie crumbs
3 tablespoons sugar
⅓ cup butter or margarine, melted
*Filling:*
3-ounce pkg. lemon gelatin
1¼ cups boiling water
8-ounce pkg. cream cheese, at room temperature
1½ cups grated apple
1 tablespoon sugar
*Topping:*
2 teaspoons cornstarch
1 tablespoon sugar
½ cup cranberry or cranapple juice
1 medium apple, peeled and thinly sliced

1. For crust: Combine crumbs, sugar, and butter; mix well. Press into 9-inch pie plate. Bake at 350 degrees 10 minutes. Cool.

2. For filling: Dissolve gelatin in 1¼ cups boiling water; add cream cheese and blend until well mixed. Refrigerate until slightly jelled. Beat again. Mix grated apple with sugar; add to gelatin mixture, blend and pour into prepared crust. Chill.

3. For topping: Mix cornstarch and sugar; add juice and heat, stirring till thickened. Add apple slices and cook till soft. Arrange slices on top of pie, pouring any remaining glaze over. Chill. Makes 1 pie.

# GRATED APPLE MERINGUE PIE

**4 large apples, grated**
**½ cup sugar**
**1 cup milk**
**2 tablespoons melted butter or margarine**
**3 eggs (reserve 2 whites for meringue)**
**½ cup raisins**
**½ teaspoon nutmeg**
**9-inch pie shell, unbaked**
**¼ cup confectioners' sugar**
**¼ cup currant or other fruit jelly**

1. Combine grated apples with sugar, milk, melted butter, one whole egg, and two of the egg yolks; blend well. Add raisins and nutmeg and pour into pie shell.

2. Bake at 350 degrees about 40 minutes, until knife inserted in custard comes out clean. Cool.

3. Make meringue: beat two egg whites till soft peaks form, add confectioners' sugar gradually and continue beating till quite stiff.

4. Spread cooled pie with jelly and then spread with meringue. Bake at 350 degrees about 10 minutes till lightly browned.
   Makes 1 pie.

*Note:* The pie is also good without jelly, but in this case a little more sugar in the pie may be needed.

# HONEY APPLE PIE

*Pastry:*
**2 cups flour**
**1 teaspoon salt**
**⅓ cup lard**
**⅓ cup margarine**
**4 to 5 tablespoons cold water**
*Filling:*
**6 medium cooking apples**
**2 tablespoons flour**
**2 teaspoons cinnamon**
**½ cup honey**
**1 ounce sherry (optional)**

1. For pastry: Place flour and salt in large bowl;
   add lard and margarine and cut in until the
   mixture is in pieces the size of peas. Add water,
   a little at a time until dough can be patted into
   two balls. Chill. Roll dough into two circles;
   line 10-inch pie plate with one circle and trim.

2. For filling: Peel, core, and slice apples. Sprinkle
   a light film of flour into prepared pie shell.
   Place one third of the apples in pie shell, sprinkle
   with a bit of flour and cinnamon; repeat twice.
   Mix honey and sherry together and drizzle
   over all.

3. Cover with top pastry crust and pierce well;
   press edges firmly together. Bake at 350 degrees
   50 minutes or until crust is golden brown. Serve
   with ice cream, if desired.
   Makes 1 pie.

# RICKRACK APPLE TART

*Pastry:*
¼ cup butter, chilled
1 cup flour
½ teaspoon salt
1 tablespoon confectioners' sugar
1 egg yolk
*Filling:*
7 tart cooking apples, pared, cored, and halved
½ cup honey
¼ cup sugar
2 tablespoons flour
½ teaspoon cinnamon
2 tablespoons butter
¼ cup cream

1. For pastry, cut butter into dry ingredients with pastry blender; stir in egg yolk. With fingertips, press dough over bottom and up on sides of 9-inch pie plate, with a ½-inch standing dough rim. With pastry wheel, roll a rickrack edge over pastry along rim of shell.

2. Slice 4 apple halves thinly into pie shell in a single layer. Combine honey, sugar, flour, and cinnamon; drizzle ½ of this mixture over apples. Arrange remaining apple halves, cut side down, in a single layer on top of apple slices. Sprinkle with remaining honey mixture; dot with butter. Pour cream in slowly near center of pie.

3. Bake at 400 degrees 1 hour. Apples will be tender, but retain their shape. Syrupy juices will thicken as pie cools. After taking pie from oven, gently press down apples very lightly into juices. Serve warm or cold.
   Makes 1 pie.

# SOUR CREAM APPLE PIE

**9-inch pie shell, unbaked**
*Filling:*
**1 cup dairy sour cream**
**2 eggs**
**2 tablespoons flour**
**½ cup sugar**
**1 teaspoon vanilla**
**4 large apples, peeled**
*Topping:*
**2 tablespoons butter, at room temperature**
**¼ cup sugar**
**1 tablespoon flour**
**½ teaspoon cinnamon**

1. For topping: Combine all ingredients with a fork. Place in refrigerator.

2. For filling: Combine sour cream, eggs, flour, sugar, and vanilla; mix well. Using slice side of a cheese grater, slice apples into sour cream mixture and fold in.

3. Pour filling into pie shell and smooth top with spoon. Crumble topping over filling. Bake at 350 degrees 1 hour.
   Makes 1 pie.

*Variation:* Arrange sliced apples in pie shell and pour sour cream mixture over. Proceed as above.

> *The fruit*
> *Of that forbidden tree,*
> *Whose mortal taste*
> *Brought death into this world, and all our woe.*
> John Milton, *Paradise Lost*

# AEBLE KAGE (APPLE CAKE)

3 pounds apples
½ cup water
¾ cup sugar
2 cups bread crumbs
2 tablespoons sugar
½ cup butter
Whipped cream (½ pint whipping cream)
Raspberry or currant jelly

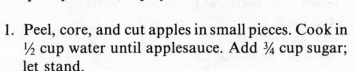

1. Peel, core, and cut apples in small pieces. Cook in ½ cup water until applesauce. Add ¾ cup sugar; let stand.

2. Mix bread crumbs with 2 tablespoons sugar. Melt butter in heavy skillet. Add crumbs and cook, stirring until browned and crisp; cool.

3. Spread a layer of crumbs in the bottom of a serving dish. Cover with a layer of applesauce. Repeat layers until all is used, ending with a layer of bread crumbs. Chill.

4. Cover top of cake with whipped cream, then dab with jelly. Use any remaining whipped cream on individual servings.
   Makes about 12 servings.

*Note:* To economize, make your own bread crumbs.

# APPLE APRICOT TORTE

1½ cups flour, sifted
1 teaspoon baking powder
2 tablespoons sugar
1 egg, slightly beaten
½ cup butter, softened
3 cups apples, peeled and finely chopped
1 cup dried apricots, cut in thin strips
1 teaspoon cinnamon
1½ cups sugar
3 eggs, slightly beaten
1 cup dairy sour cream
¼ cup almonds, finely chopped

1. Sift flour, baking powder, and 2 tablespoons sugar together. Add egg and butter; work into flour mixture until a smooth dough is formed. Press dough into a thin layer on the bottom and sides of a buttered 9-inch springform pan, making the sides 2 inches high.

2. Combine apples, apricots, cinnamon, and 1½ cups sugar. Combine eggs and sour cream; blend until smooth. Add to apple mixture and mix well.

3. Pour into dough-lined pan and sprinkle with the almonds. Bake at 350 degrees for 1 hour and 15 minutes. Cool and remove from pan. Makes 12 servings.

*Apples are best stored in the refrigerator where decay is prevented and quality, juiciness, and crispness are maintained.*

# APPLE BAKED ALASKA

5 apples, pared, cored, and thinly sliced
3 tablespoons sugar
2 teaspoons cornstarch
½ teaspoon each nutmeg and cinnamon
¼ teaspoon salt
1 quart vanilla ice cream
3 egg whites
⅛ teaspoon cream of tartar
¼ cup confectioners' sugar

1. Arrange sliced apples in 9-inch pie plate.
   Combine sugar, cornstarch, spices, and salt;
   sprinkle evenly over apples. Cover with
   aluminum foil; bake in 425 degree oven
   30 minutes or until apples are just tender.
   Remove from oven, cool, and refrigerate.

2. At serving time, cover with even layer of ice
   cream; place in freezer.

3. Meanwhile, beat egg whites with cream of tartar
   till frothy. Gradually add confectioners' sugar,
   a tablespoon at a time, and continue beating until
   mixture stands in peaks.

4. Spread meringue over ice cream (spread to rim of
   pie plate so that edges are sealed). Place pie plate
   in roasting pan, and surround pie plate with
   ice cubes to keep cold. Bake in 500 degree oven
   3 minutes until lightly browned.
   Makes 8 to 10 servings.

*Note:* If time permits, keep apples covered with ice
cream in freezer until ice cream is really hardened,
and apples well chilled.

# APPLE BONNIE

**6 large apples (McIntosh preferred)**
**1 tablespoon fresh lemon juice**
**½ pound margarine or butter**
**1 pkg. (2 layer size) yellow cake mix**
**½ cup flaked coconut**
**1 dozen marshmallows**

1. Peel, core, and slice apples. Arrange in a
   13 x 9 x 2-inch pan. Sprinkle lemon juice
   over apples.

2. Blend margarine into dry cake mix until crumbly,
   mix in coconut and sprinkle over top of apples.

3. Place the marshmallows over top of cake mix
   about 2 inches apart.

4. Bake at 350 degrees about 40 minutes. To serve,
   cut in squares.
   Makes 28 squares.

*There are over 8000 named apple varieties in history.*
*More than 2500 are in America.*

# APPLE CHEESE CAKE

**4 ounces cream cheese**
**½ cup butter or margarine**
**1 egg**
**¾ cup sugar**
**1 cup flour, sifted**
**1 teaspoon baking powder**
**3 apples, pared and sliced**
**½ cup brown sugar**
**1 teaspoon cinnamon**

1. Beat the cream cheese and butter until creamy. Add the egg and sugar and beat until very fluffy.

2. Sift flour and baking powder, and gently fold into cheese mixture.

3. Put into a deep 9-inch pie plate which has been well greased and dusted with flour.

4. Cover the top with apple slices in a pinwheel shape.

5. Sprinkle with a mixture of brown sugar and cinnamon. Bake at 350 degrees for 40 to 45 minutes.

6. Serve warm with sweetened whipped cream.

*Note:* Maple sugar makes an elegant substitute for brown sugar.

# DIET BREAKER DESSERT

1 egg, beaten
2 tablespoons flour
½ cup maple or maple flavored syrup
1 cup sour cream
½ teaspoon maple flavoring
4 cups apples, peeled and sliced
*Topping:*
1 cup butter or margarine
1 cup brown sugar
1 egg
1½ cups all-purpose flour
1 teaspoon baking soda
½ teaspoon salt
1 cup sour cream
½ teaspoon maple flavoring

1. Mix beaten egg well with 2 tablespoons flour, maple syrup, sour cream, maple flavoring, and apples. Spoon into greased 10-inch pan.

2. For topping, cream butter and sugar; add egg and cream until light and fluffy. Sift dry ingredients, add to creamed mixture along with sour cream and maple flavoring; beat until smooth.

3. Pour topping onto apple mixture. Bake in 350 degree oven about 45 minutes. Serve with cream or ice cream. Makes 9 to 12 servings.

*Coleridge holds that a man cannot have a pure mind who refuses apple dumplings.*
Charles Lamb, *Grace Before Meat*

✓

# APPLE POUND CAKE

*325° oven*

*1 wheat*
**3 cups flour, unsifted**
1 teaspoon baking soda
1 teaspoon salt
1 teaspoon cinnamon
*1 c. brown*
**1½ cups corn oil**
*1 wht*
**2 cups white sugar**
3 eggs
2 teaspoons vanilla
2 cups pared and shredded apples
1 cup finely chopped pecans
½ cup butter or margarine
½ cup light brown sugar, firmly packed
2 teaspoons milk

1. Grease and flour a 10x4-inch bundt pan.

2. Thoroughly stir together the flour, baking soda, salt, and cinnamon.

3. In a large bowl, beat together at medium speed on the mixer, the oil, white sugar, eggs, and vanilla until combined. Gradually beat in flour mixture until smooth. Fold in apples and pecans. Turn into prepared pan.

4. Bake in preheated 325 degree oven for 1 hour and 20 minutes. Place cake in pan on a wire rack to cool for 20 minutes.

5. About 5 minutes before cake has finished cooling, in a small saucepan, stirring constantly, bring the butter, brown sugar, and milk to a boil; boil 2 minutes.

6. With a small spatula, loosen cake edges and around tube. Turn out on rack. At once spoon the hot sugar mixture over the still warm cake, allowing it to run down the sides. Cool completely. (For a day or two, cake may be stored in a tightly covered tin; for longer storage, cover and refrigerate, but bring to room temperature before serving.)
Makes 1 cake.

*Since apples keep longer than most other fruits, it's frequently economical to buy them in large amounts. They should be stored in a cool, well ventilated cellar or on a sheltered back porch. The cooler the storage area the better, but temperature should not go below freezing. Store only good apples, as one bad one will spoil the entire lot.*

# BAVARIAN APPLE ALMOND TORTE

*Torte:*
½ cup butter or margarine
1½ cups blanched almonds
3 eggs
1 cup sugar
2 tablespoons flour

1. Butter a 9-inch cake pan. Line with waxed paper and butter the paper.

2. Cream butter until very light and fluffy. Grind almonds in blender until fine.

3. Beat eggs and sugar until foamy. Alternately add creamed butter and ground almonds to eggs and sugar, mixing well after each addition. Stir in flour and pour into pan.

4. Bake at 350 degrees for 30 to 35 minutes. Turn out onto rack and cool. Place on serving dish upside down, remove paper and spread on prepared custard.

*Custard:*
¼ cup sugar
1 tablespoon cornstarch
¼ teaspoon salt
1 cup milk
1 egg yolk, beaten
1 tablespoon butter
½ teaspoon almond flavoring

1. Combine sugar, cornstarch, and salt in a saucepan. Slowly stir in milk. Bring to a boil, stirring constantly, boil 1 minute.

2. Stir half of the mixture into egg yolk. Blend into remaining mixture and cook for 1 more minute. Remove from heat; stir in butter and almond flavoring. Cool and spread over torte. Refrigerate torte.

*Apple Topping:*
**3 red-skinned apples**
**3 tablespoons butter**
**1 tablespoon brown sugar**
**2 tablespoons red jelly (currant or other)**

1. Core and cut apples into 9 ½-inch slices, discarding end pieces. Brown 3 tablespoons butter with the brown sugar in a large skillet. Sauté apple slices on both sides until just soft.

2. Cool slightly, arrange overlapping slices on top of custard. Melt jelly and spoon over apples. Serves 8 to 10.

*The friendly cow all red and white*
*I love with all my heart;*
*She gives me cream with all her might*
*To eat with apple tarte.*
Robert Louis Stevenson
*A Child's Garden of Verses*

# DUTCH APPLE CAKE

2½ cups sifted flour
2 teaspoons baking powder
2 tablespoons sugar
1 cup butter
1 teaspoon vanilla
1 egg, slightly beaten
6 medium sized cooking apples
*Topping:*
1½ cups sugar
2½ tablespoons flour
½ teaspoon salt
¼ cup butter
1 teaspoon cinnamon

1. Sift together flour, baking powder, and sugar. Cut in butter until mixture is crumbly.

2. Add vanilla to egg; blend with flour mixture. Press evenly onto bottom and sides of 15x10x1-inch pan.

3. Arrange peeled, sliced apples in overlapping layers to cover dough. Combine topping ingredients; sprinkle over apples.

4. Bake at 350 degrees for 45 minutes, or until apples are tender and topping is golden brown.

5. Cut into squares; serve warm or cold with whipped cream or orange sauce.
   Makes 12 large servings or 16 smaller.

*Orange Sauce:*
**1 cup sugar**
**2 tablespoons cornstarch**
**1 teaspoon salt**
**1 cup water**
**2 tablespoons butter**
**6-ounce can orange juice concentrate, undiluted**

1. Combine the sugar, cornstarch, and salt in a saucepan. Add water slowly, stirring constantly. Add butter and bring to a boil. Reduce heat and continue cooking until mixture thickens. Remove from heat and stir in orange juice concentrate.

2. Serve warm or chilled on hot Dutch Apple Cake.

*Note:* For apple sauce, substitute 1 cup apple juice for water; eliminate orange juice. Or make with lemonade concentrate and omit sugar.

*Massachusetts Governor John Endicott planted the first nursery of fruit trees at Danvers, Massachusetts.*

# GODDESS TRIBUTE

6 tablespoons butter
3 tablespoons sugar
2 egg yolks
¾ cup plus 2 tablespoons flour, sifted
6 tablespoons blanched almonds, finely cut
3 tablespoons lemon rind, shredded
5 tablespoons sugar
2 tablespoons lemon juice
5 apples, pared, halved, and cored
6 tablespoons raspberry jam
4 egg whites
Dash salt
½ cup sugar

1. Cream butter and 3 tablespoons sugar together.
   Add egg yolks and beat vigorously. Stir in flour,
   almonds, and lemon rind; blend well. Press
   dough on the bottom of an 8-inch square pan.
   Brush with slightly beaten egg white (use a small
   amount of egg white from which meringue is
   made). Bake at 350 degrees for 15 minutes or
   until crust is golden brown. Cool in pan.

2. Meanwhile, combine the 5 tablespoons sugar and
   lemon juice in skillet. Add apple halves, cover
   tightly and cook over low heat until apples are
   just tender. Spread cooled crust with jam, then
   arrange apples on top.

3. Beat egg whites and salt until frothy; add
   remaining sugar gradually, beating constantly;
   continue beating until peaks are formed. Pile
   meringue lightly over apples. Bake at 350 degrees
   for 15 minutes. Makes 9 to 12 servings.

# QUICK APPLE KUCHEN

¼ lb. margarine or butter
1 pkg. (2 layer size) yellow cake mix
½ cup flaked coconut
6 large sized apples
½ cup sugar
1 teaspoon cinnamon
2 egg yolks or 1 whole egg
1 cup dairy sour cream

1. Cut margarine into dry cake mix until crumbly. Mix in coconut. Pat into 13 x 9 x 2-inch pan; build up edge slightly. Bake in preheated 350 degree oven 10 minutes.

3. Meanwhile, core apples; peel and slice thinly. Arrange on warm crust after baking. Mix sugar and cinnamon; sprinkle on apples.

4. Beat egg and mix with sour cream; spread over apples. Bake in 350 degree oven 25 minutes or until apples are cooked through. Do not over-bake. Makes 1 cake, about 15 servings.

*When Eve upon the first of men*
*The apple pressed with specious cant*
*Oh! What a thousand pities then*
*That Adam was not Adamant.*
Thomas Hood, *A Reflection*

# SHERRY APPLE CAKE SUPERB

1 cup butter or margarine
2 cups sugar
3 eggs
3 cups flour
1½ teaspoons baking soda
½ teaspoon salt
1 teaspoon cinnamon
⅛ teaspoon nutmeg
3 cups peeled and chopped apples
2 cups chopped walnuts or pecans
2 teaspoons vanilla

1. Cream the butter and sugar well. Add the eggs, one at a time, beating well after each addition.

2. Combine dry ingredients, sift and add gradually, mixing until well blended. Add apples, nuts, and vanilla.

3. Pour into greased and floured bundt pan or 10-inch tube pan. Bake in preheated 325 degree oven 1½ hours or until cake tester inserted in center of cake comes out clean. Let stand 15 minutes; then remove from pan.

4. For glaze: Combine 1½ cups sugar, ¼ cup butter, and ½ cup sherry in small saucepan. Mix and stir over low heat until butter melts and sugar dissolves.

5. With a fork, prick the cake well all over. Slowly pour the glaze all over cake until it absorbs all the glaze. Makes 1 cake.

# NOTES

# APPLE DESSERTS

Baked Apples
Cookies
Crêpes
Puddings
Confections

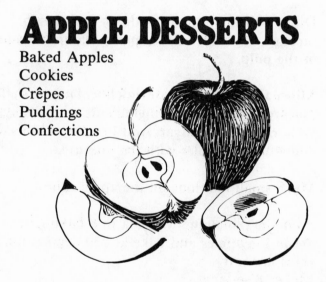

# RICOTTA STUFFED APPLES

**8 baking apples**
**½ cup almonds, peeled**
**2 ounces sweet or unsweetened chocolate**
**8 Amaretti or small macaroons**
**1 egg yolk**
**10 tablespoons ricotta cheese**
**6 tablespoons sugar**
**3 ounces Marsala wine**

1. Dig a well three-quarters down each apple through the core; with a spoon, scoop out some of the pulp.

2. Mince the almonds, grate the chocolate, crush the macaroons. Mix these ingredients with the egg yolk, ricotta, and sugar. Add 1 ounce of Marsala and stuff the apples with the mixture.

3. Make small incisions on the apple skins.

4. Pour the remaining Marsala in a baking dish. Set in the apples and bake at 350 degrees until skins are soft.
   Makes 8 servings.

# APPLE BLOSSOM

**4 medium sized baking apples**
**²/₃ cup raisins**
**²/₃ cup chopped pecans**
**3 tablespoons sherry or orange juice**
**½ cup brown sugar**
**Butter or margarine**
**Whipped cream**

1. Grease 4 medium sized custard dishes. Core, then peel apples (not all the way down, creating a petal effect). Mix together raisins, chopped pecans, and sherry to taste. Spoon mixture inside area created by petals.

2. Sprinkle top generously with brown sugar and a good sized piece of butter.

3. Bake at 350 degrees until apples are just done, not too hard or too soft.

4. When ready to serve, top with whipped cream, and if desired, sprinkle with candied red sugar. Makes 4 servings.

*Most apples are marketed by grade which is determined by their color, maturity, lack of defects, and general appearance. U.S. grades for apples are U.S. Extra Fancy, U.S. Fancy, U.S. No. 1 and combinations of these grades. U.S. No. 2 is a less desirable grade.*

# APPLE DUMPLINGS

2 cups flour
2 teaspoons baking powder
1 teaspoon salt
1 tablespoon sugar
2 tablespoons butter or margarine
2/3 cup milk
6 baking apples
1/2 cup sugar
1 teaspoon nutmeg

1. Sift dry ingredients together; cut in butter until mixture is slightly coarser than cornmeal. Mix in milk quickly with fork, adding more if necessary so dough holds together.

2. Pat out and roll lightly on floured board to about 1/4-inch thickness into rectangle about 10 by 15 inches. Cut into six 5x5-inch squares.

3. Place each apple on a square; sprinkle with combined sugar and nutmeg. Draw four corners of dough together on top of each apple and pinch edges together. Prick with fork and bake in 350 degree oven for 30 to 45 minutes until lightly browned. Makes 6 servings.

*Variations:* Fill center of apples with homemade or canned whole cranberry sauce. When serving, top with hot cranberry sauce, thinned slightly with water and seasoned with nutmeg and cloves if desired.

*Greek and Roman myths refer to apples as symbols of love and beauty.*

# APPLE FONDUE FRITTERS

Fondue pot and fondue forks
1 cup pancake mix
2 tablespoons cornflake crumbs
1 tablespoon sugar
⅛ teaspoon curry powder (optional)
¾ cup water
Cooking oil
4 medium apples, pared, cored, and sliced
2 teaspoons cinnamon mixed with ½ cup sugar

1. Combine pancake mix, cornflake crumbs, sugar, and curry powder. Add water to dry mixture and beat well until smooth. Pour batter into individual serving bowls.

2. Pour cooking oil into fondue pot until half full. Heat to 375 degrees. Spear apple slice with fondue fork. Dip into batter, drain excess batter over bowl. Place apple slice in hot oil and cook 1 to 2 minutes till golden brown. Dip into cinnamon and sugar mixture. Repeat process. Makes 4 to 6 servings.

*William Tell became famous by shooting an apple off his son's head at the order of some invaders of Switzerland.*

# APPLE DATE SQUARES

½ cup shortening or margarine
¾ cup sugar
1 egg
1½ cups sifted flour
1 teaspoon baking soda
¼ teaspoon salt
2 cups finely chopped apples
1 cup cut up dates
*Topping:*
¼ cup brown sugar
1 teaspoon cinnamon
½ cup chopped nuts

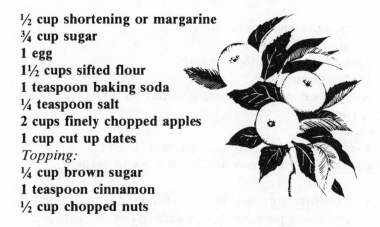

1. Cream shortening and sugar; add egg and beat well. Sift flour, baking soda, and salt; add to creamed mixture and blend.

2. Stir in fruits; spread in greased 9-inch square baking dish. Combine ingredients for topping; sprinkle evenly over the apple mixture.

3. Bake in 350 degree oven 30 to 35 minutes. Cut in squares. May be served warm with vanilla ice cream. Makes 16 squares.

*The first commercial apple nursery was established in Flushing, New York (on Long Island) in 1730.*

# APPLE BUTTERSCOTCH SQUARES

2 or 3 large apples, peeled
½ cup shortening
¾ cup brown sugar
2 eggs
½ cup sour cream
½ cup milk
1 teaspoon vanilla
2 cups flour
1 teaspoon baking soda
Dash of salt
1 pkg. (6 oz.) butterscotch bits

1. Cut up apples, remove seeds and grate (or grate in blender).

2. Cream shortening and sugar; blend in eggs, sour cream, milk, and vanilla. Sift dry ingredients together and mix with shortening mixture.

3. Add grated apples and butterscotch bits. Spread into greased 9-inch square baking pan. Bake at 350 degrees for about 45 minutes or until browned lightly. Cut into squares.
   Makes 25 squares.

*Smooth apple: One who is or thinks he is suave or charming.*

# APPLE HERMITS

1 cup sugar
½ cup salad oil
3 cups flour
1½ teaspoons cinnamon
½ teaspoon nutmeg
½ teaspoon salt
1 teaspoon baking soda
¼ cup molasses
¼ cup black coffee
½ cup milk
1 cup diced apples
¾ cup raisins
Sugar

1. Cream 1 cup sugar and the salad oil. Sift together the dry ingredients. Add alternately with the molasses, coffee, and milk.

2. Fold in apples and raisins. The batter will be stiff; spread in strips across two greased cookie sheets. Bake in 350 degree oven for 20 to 25 minutes.

3. Dust with sugar while still warm; cut in squares. Makes about 40 hermits.

# APPLE RAISIN COOKIES

½ cup shortening
1 ⅓ cups brown sugar
1 egg
2 cups flour
½ teaspoon salt
1 teaspoon baking soda
½ cup milk
1 cup unpared apples, finely chopped
1 cup raisins
1 cup nuts, chopped (optional)
Vanilla Glaze (recipe follows)

1. Cream shortening, sugar, and egg. Combine the dry ingredients; add half and then blend in milk. Add remaining dry ingredients. Mix well.

2. Add apples, raisins, and nuts; mix. Drop by teaspoonfuls on greased cookie sheet; bake at 350 degrees for 10 to 12 minutes.

3. Vanilla Glaze: Combine 1½ cups confectioners' sugar, 4 teaspoons milk, 1 teaspoon melted butter, ¼ teaspoon vanilla, and dash of salt. Mix until creamy; spread on cookies.
   Makes about 4 dozen cookies.

*The secret to moist cookies is to keep an apple in the cookie jar.*

# BUTTERY CARAMEL APPLE SQUARES

11-ounce pkg. pie crust mix
½ cup granulated brown sugar
1 cup quick cooking oatmeal, uncooked
¾ cup walnuts, chopped
3 tablespoons butter, melted
¼ cup cold water
2 tablespoons cornstarch
3 tablespoons sugar
4 medium cooking apples, pared, cored, and shredded
12-ounce jar caramel topping

1. Place oven rack in second position from bottom; preheat oven to 375 degrees. Very lightly grease 13x9x2-inch baking pan on bottom and 1 inch up sides.

2. Combine pie crust mix, brown sugar, oats, and nuts; drizzle with 2 tablespoons of butter and the water. Stir with fork until evenly combined. Reserve 1½ cups of this mixture.

3. Press remaining crumb mixture into prepared pan, covering bottom of pan and ¼ inch up sides.

4. Sprinkle cornstarch and sugar over apples; stir to combine. Spoon apples evenly over crust. Combine 1 tablespoon butter with caramel topping; drizzle over apples. Crumble reserved crumb mixture evenly over apples.

5. Bake for 35 to 40 minutes until topping is golden brown. When cool, cut in 2-inch squares. Makes 24 squares.

# DIVINE APPLE SQUARES

2½ cups sifted flour
1 cup plus 1 tablespoon sugar
1 teaspoon salt
1 cup shortening
1 egg, separated
Milk
⅔ cup crushed cornflakes
4 cups peeled and sliced apples
1½ teaspoons cinnamon, to taste
1 cup confectioners' sugar
2 tablespoons lemon juice

1. Sift flour, 1 tablespoon sugar, and salt together; cut in shortening. Place egg yolk in measuring cup; add milk to make ⅓ cup liquid. Add to shortening mixture; mix just enough for dough to shape into ball.

2. Roll out half to 15x11-inch rectangle; transfer to rimmed baking sheet. Cover with cornflakes; spread with apples. Mix remaining sugar with cinnamon; sprinkle over apples.

3. Roll remaining dough for top crust; place over apples, pinching edges together. Cut steam vents in crust. Beat egg white until stiff; spread on top crust. Bake in 400 degree oven for 40 minutes.

4. Combine confectioners' sugar and lemon juice to make glaze. Drizzle over hot crust. Cut into squares. Makes 16 servings.

*Note:* This recipe freezes beautifully and can also be cut into small squares for afternoon teas.

# APPLE STUFFED CRÊPES

*Crêpes:*
**2 eggs**
**2 tablespoons salad oil**
**1 cup milk**
**¾ cup sifted flour**
**½ teaspoon salt**
**2 tablespoons sugar**
**½ teaspoon brandy extract**
*Filling:*
**2 pounds tart cooking apples**
**½ cup water**
**¾ cup finely chopped walnuts**
**1 teaspoon lemon juice**
**¼ teaspoon cinnamon**
**¼ teaspoon nutmeg**
**½ cup maple syrup**
**Sugar to taste**

**Butter to cook crêpes**
**Confectioners' sugar**

1. Crêpes: In medium bowl, beat together eggs, oil, and milk. Add remaining ingredients and beat until very smooth. Refrigerate, covered, for at least an hour.

2. Filling: Peel and slice apples. Place in saucepan with water, walnuts, lemon juice, cinnamon, and nutmeg. Bring to boil; reduce heat and simmer covered, approximately 20 minutes. Add maple syrup and sugar, if desired. Cook until mixture is very thick. Keep warm.

3. In 7-inch skillet, melt 1 teaspoon butter over medium heat. When butter is hot, add 1½

tablespoons batter, rotating pan quickly to cover bottom. Cook one minute on each side or until golden brown. Repeat with remaining batter. Keep crêpes warm in oven.

4. Place about 3 tablespoons apple filling on each crêpe and lightly spread over crêpe. Roll up crêpes and place on warm serving dish. Sprinkle with confectioners' sugar. Serve warm.
Makes 20 crêpes.

> *My apple tree will never get across*
> *And eat the cones under his pines,*
> *I tell him.*
> *He only says,*
> *"Good fences make good neighbors."*
> Robert Frost
> *Mending Walls*

# RICOTTA APPLE ROLL-UPS
## with Apple Applesauce

*Crêpes:*
1½ cups flour
1 tablespoon sugar
2 teaspoons baking powder
½ teaspoon salt
1 egg, beaten thick
1½ cups milk
2 tablespoons butter, melted and cooled
1 large apple, peeled and grated
½ teaspoon vanilla
Butter to cook crêpes
*Filling:*
2 cups ricotta cheese
1 cup sour cream
2 teaspoons sugar
*Apple Applesauce:*
4 medium apples, peeled and quartered
¼ cup sugar
¼ cup pineapple juice
Nutmeg

1. Crêpes: Sift together dry ingredients. Combine egg, milk, melted butter, and grated apple. Add liquid mixture to dry mixture and beat with rotary beater until smooth. Add vanilla.

2. Grease a 6-inch skillet lightly with butter and spoon ¼ cup batter into skillet. Spread batter quickly with spoon. Cook over medium heat until lightly browned. Flip crêpe and brown on other side. Repeat with rest of batter. Keep crêpes warm in 300 degree oven.

3. Filling: Combine ricotta cheese, sour cream, and

sugar. Drop about 3 tablespoons of filling into the center of each crêpe. Roll up crêpes and place on warm serving dish.

4. Apple Applesauce: Place apples, sugar, and pineapple juice in a blender. Mix until thick sauce is formed. Pour into saucepan and bring to a boil. Pour sauce over crêpes or serve separately. Dust with nutmeg. Makes 12.

# APPLE INDIAN PUDDING

½ cup yellow cornmeal
1 quart milk, scalded
⅔ cup molasses
1 teaspoon cinnamon or ginger
1 teaspoon salt
2 tart apples, pared and sliced
2 cups cold milk

1. Add cornmeal slowly to hot milk in double boiler. Cook, stirring constantly until thick. Add molasses, cinnamon, and salt.

2. Place alternate layers of mixture and apples into buttered baking dish. Pour cold milk on top. Bake at 300 degrees, 2 hours or longer. Serve with hard sauce or vanilla ice cream, if desired. Makes 8 to 10 servings.

# APPLE COBBLER

4 cups peeled and sliced baking apples
1 cup sugar
⅛ teaspoon cinnamon
½ teaspoon almond extract (optional)
2 tablespoons butter
1½ cups sifted flour
2 teaspoons baking powder
⅓ cup sugar
½ teaspoon salt
¼ cup butter
1 egg, beaten
⅔ cup milk

1. Place apples in 1½-quart baking dish. Sprinkle with 1 cup sugar, cinnamon, and almond extract; dot with 2 tablespoons butter.

2. Sift flour, baking powder, ⅓ cup sugar and salt into mixing bowl. Cut in ¼ cup butter until mixture is slightly coarser than cornmeal.

3. Combine egg and milk; pour into dry ingredients and blend just enough to combine. Spoon this over apples in baking dish.

4. Bake in 425 degree oven about 30 minutes or until browned. Serve with fresh cream, sour cream, or ice cream if desired.
   Makes 6 to 8 servings.

*Apples help clean the teeth and provide roughage; they are also high in potassium, low in sodium, and provide a source of natural sugar.*

# APPLE KUGEL

½ pound fine noodles, cooked and rinsed
¼ pound margarine, melted
2 apples, peeled and sliced
3 eggs, lightly beaten
½ cup dark corn syrup
½ cup golden raisins
⅓ cup sugar
½ teaspoon cinnamon
1 teaspoon vanilla
⅓ cup orange juice
1 tablespoon lemon juice
½ cup cornflake crumbs

*Crumb topping:*
⅔ cup cornflake crumbs
⅔ cup sugar
1 teaspoon cinnamon
½ cup crushed walnuts

1. Mix all ingredients together except crumbs and crumb topping.

2. Grease 7½x13-inch pyrex pan. Sprinkle with ½ cup cornflake crumbs. Pour noodle mixture into pan.

3. Combine ingredients for crumb topping. Sprinkle over kugel.

4. Bake at 350 degrees for 30 minutes. Serve hot or cold. Makes 12 to 16 servings.

*Note:* Graham cracker crumbs may be used instead of cornflake crumbs.

# APPLE NOODLE PUDDING

½ pound wide egg noodles
3 eggs, beaten
4 tablespoons melted butter
¼ cup sugar
½ teaspoon salt
½ cup sour cream
1 cup milk
½ teaspoon vanilla
4 ounces farmers' cheese
½ pound cottage cheese
3 ounces cream cheese
1½ cups apples, cut up
Cinnamon and brown sugar
Butter

1. Cook noodles. Beat eggs with butter, sugar, salt, sour cream, milk, and vanilla. Mix cheeses together (soften first). Add to egg mixture. Mix well and add noodles. Stir in cut up apples. Pour into 13x9x2-inch pan.

2. Bake at 350 degrees for 45 minutes, then sprinkle top with cinnamon and brown sugar to taste and dot surface with butter. Bake ½ hour longer. Cool and cut into squares. Serve warm. May also be served with spoonful of sour cream on top. Makes 18 servings.

*My heart is like an apple tree*
*Whose boughs are bent with thick-set fruit.*
D. G. Rossetti,
*A Birthday*

# APPLE SUPREME

**4 tart apples, peeled and grated**
**½ cup sugar**
**¼ cup butter or margarine**
**¼ teaspoon salt**
**3 eggs, separated**
**2 tablespoons lemon juice**

1. Cream sugar and butter together. Add salt and egg yolks and beat until well blended. Add the lemon juice, a little at a time, and then the grated apples.

2. Beat egg whites until stiff; fold into apple mixture and pour into a greased casserole and bake at 350 degrees for 35 to 40 minutes.

3. This is best served with whipped cream, but may also be served with fresh or frozen strawberries or plain cream.
   Makes 5 or 6 servings.

*It was from out the rind of one apple tasted*
*That the knowledge of good and evil*
*As two twins cleaving together*
*Leaped forth into the world.*
Milton,
*Areopogitica*

# FRESH APPLE MOUSSE

½ cup sugar
½ cup water
½ teaspoon vanilla extract
2 cups apples, pared and sliced
½ pint heavy cream
1 tablespoon sugar
1 teaspoon vanilla extract
1½ cups peanut brittle, crushed

1. Combine ½ cup sugar, water, and ½ teaspoon vanilla in saucepan. Bring to a slow boil. Add apple slices and simmer slowly until tender and transparent, 2 to 5 minutes. Remove apple slices from syrup, let cool.

2. Whip cream, adding remaining sugar and vanilla. Fold apple slices carefully into whipped cream.

3. Using parfait glasses, spoon a layer of the apple cream mixture and sprinkle with a little peanut brittle. Repeat layers, topping with crushed peanut brittle. Chill in refrigerator 4 to 5 hours or overnight. Makes 4 to 6 servings.

*Send kisses with apples, and I will feast with pleasure.*
Petronius

# FRUIT NOODLE PUDDING

1 pound egg noodles
¼ pound margarine
8 apples, peeled and sliced
1 can (16 oz.) whole cranberry sauce
3 tablespoons sugar, cinnamon to taste
About ½ cup cornflake crumbs
Sugar and cinnamon to taste
4 eggs
2 cups pineapple juice

1. Cook noodles according to package directions. Drain and add margarine. Place ⅓ noodles in greased 13x9x2-inch pan. Add ½ apples, ½ cranberry sauce and sprinkle with combined sugar and cinnamon.

2. Layer ⅓ noodles, then remaining apples, cranberry sauce, sugar, and cinnamon. Add last layer of noodles; cover with cornflake crumbs combined with sugar and cinnamon.

3. Beat eggs; add pineapple juice. Spoon over noodles. Bake at 350 degrees for 1¼ hours. Makes 10 to 16 servings.

*In early 20th century New Orleans, apples were used as magic objects in voodoo ceremonies when love was the object.*

# CANDIED APPLES

**6 small well-colored apples**
**6 wooden skewers**
**1 cup sugar**
**½ cup water**
**Red food coloring (optional)**

1. Remove stems from apples and insert skewers.
   (If stems are sturdy, apples may be candied
   without skewers.)

2. Cook sugar and water until brittle when tried in
   cold water, or until candy thermometer registers
   265 degrees F. Remove from heat and stir in
   a few drops of food coloring if desired.

3. Dip each apple into sugar syrup, coating well.
   Cool on buttered cooking sheet until coating
   is set. Makes 6 candied apples.

*Adam was but human —*
*this explains it all.*
*He did not want the apple*
*for the apple's sake;*
*he wanted it only*
*because it was forbidden.*
Mark Twain,
*Pudd'nhead Wilson's Calendar*

# CRYSTALLIZED APPLE SLICES

**3 firm apples**
**1 cup sugar**
**½ cup water**

1. Peel, quarter, and core apples. Cut each quarter into 3 slices.

2. Cook sugar and water to a syrup in small saucepan. Drop 12 apple slices in syrup and cook slowly until transparent. Repeat until all are cooked.

3. Remove to wax paper and cool 24 hours. Roll in granulated sugar and repeat every 24 hours, until after third rolling, let dry.
   Makes 36 slices.

*Note:* If desired, syrup may be flavored with cinnamon or mint.

*Apple knockers: All persons who live west of the Hudson River and north or east of the Bronx.*

Al Smith,
Presidential Candidate, 1928

# OLD-FASHIONED APPLE CANDY

8 large tart apples
½ cup water
2 cups sugar
⅔ cup red cinnamon candies
1 tablespoon (1 envelope) unflavored gelatin
¼ cup cold water
Sugar

1. Quarter and core apples; add ½ cup water. Cover tightly. Cook until tender. Sieve. This should make 4 cups applesauce.

2. Add sugar and cinnamon candies. Simmer, uncovered, 45 minutes.

3. Soften gelatin in ¼ cup cold water. Add to hot mixture. Cook 20 minutes, stirring constantly. Pour into greased 8-inch square pan. Cool.

4. Cut into squares, dip in granulated or confectioners' sugar. Store in cool place. Let stand 1 day. Makes 64 pieces.

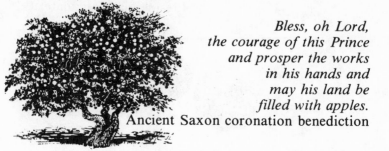

*Bless, oh Lord,
the courage of this Prince
and prosper the works
in his hands and
may his land be
filled with apples.*
Ancient Saxon coronation benediction

# NOTES

# INDEX

## A

# G

# H

# I

# J

# K

# M

# NOTES

# NOTES

# NOTES